Perfect Freedom

Brian Mountford

Why liberal Christianity might
be the faith you're looking for

Alan

with Thanks + Best wishes

Brian

John Hunt
Publishing Limited

Copyright © 2003 John Hunt Publishing Ltd
46A West Street, Alresford, Hants SO24 9AU, UK
Tel: +44 (0) 1962 736880   Fax: +44 (0) 1962 736881
E-mail: office@johnhunt-publishing.com
www.johnhunt-publishing.com

Text: © Brian Mountford 2003
Cover: Nautilus Design, UK
Typography: Jim Weaver Design

ISBN 1 84298 112 9

A CIP catalogue record for this book is available from the British Library.

Printed in the UK by Ashford Colour Press

To Annette with gratitude

Contents

1.
Liberal Christianity

'Liberal' is not a word I enthusiastically choose to describe my Christian faith because it is open to so many criticisms, but it's hard to find a better one. Liberal Christianity is criticised for its rose-tinted optimism about human nature and taken to task for its intellectual and moral tolerance, which some accuse of being so inclusive that anything goes, anything is acceptable – even irreligion! And on moral matters it is said that it compromises with the spirit of the age, allowing moral relativism in place of God's moral authority. The critical *coup de grace* is the claim that liberalism prospers in a stable society where there is economic growth, suggesting that it is a decadent religion.

Well, opponents would say that, wouldn't they? I accept that each of these strictures holds some water, but they are criticisms that can also be levelled against other Christian traditions. For example, is any moral tradition in practice able to isolate itself from the influence of the society and culture in which it is embedded?

My problem is that I have much in common with liberals but don't recognise myself in the typical textbook definition of liberalism. So, if not an out and out liberal, what? A better description of the Christianity I love and admire might be *Christianity Unchained*. Unchained from what? In a nutshell unchained from Biblical, moral, and churchy fundamentalism and their immediate derivatives. Which means that when I read the Bible I am free to explore its poetry without being castigated for not taking it literally; when I think about right and wrong I am free to consider the spirit rather than the letter of the law; and when I go to church I am free from obsessions about the details of ritual.

But it's *freedom* not *anarchy* I want, which might come as a bit of a surprise to those who accuse me of letting 'anything go' or of being 'all questions and no answers'. There's shape and order to my Christianity, but it's shape and order designed to liberate the believer. You might draw an analogy between this and the rigidity of the human skeleton, which in conjunction with the flesh and muscles gives freedom of movement to the individual. If you have only a rigid framework then you have a cumbersome, restricted, and inflexible body that becomes its own prisoner. This is what the prophet Ezekiel recognised when he spoke of the Valley of the Dry Bones, when God said to the bones: I will lay sinews on you, and will cause flesh to come upon you, and put breath in you, and you shall live.

My theological underpinning for Christianity Unchained is located in three images. The first is the generosity or prodigality of God, illustrated by two of Jesus' parables: the Sower and the Prodigal Son. The sower casts the seed of the gospel with extravagant open-handedness over the good ground, the stony ground, the path and among the thorns, showing no discrimination and knowing that only such apparently reckless sowing will bring results. The same spirit of generosity is shown by the father of the Prodigal Son. He has been exploited by his son, who has squandered his inheritance while travelling abroad, but when the son returns, instead of being censorious, he welcomes him by giving him fine clothes, a ring on his finger and a massive homecoming party.

The second theological underpinning is an impression I have of Jesus typified by his dislike of hypocrisy and showy religion – if you're fasting, don't disfigure your face; when you make a donation do it anonymously. The whole sense that one gets of Jesus as a rebellious, non-establishment, creative, exploratory man who chose simple fishermen as his closest disciples and told the clergy that the Sabbath was made for man not man for the Sabbath. This was a prophetic and enigmatic character with a liking for the wilderness, and an openness to publicans, sinners, social outcasts and women (in a society that afforded women very few rights). So Jesus was happy to break boundaries and social conventions; he said as much in his opening sermon in the synagogue in Nazareth when he emphasised good news to the poor and freedom for the captives.

My third theological underpinning is summed up by a phrase from Morning Prayer, which provides the title for this book, 'Whose service is perfect freedom'. To put it in context the prayer begins: 'O God who art the author of peace and lover of concord, in knowledge of whom standeth our eternal life, whose service is perfect freedom.' It is a paradoxical idea to be sure because 'service' or slavery would appear to be the opposite of freedom, but it is the backbone of Christian liberalism. This is the idea that to follow God's values is liberating not restricting. God expects his creatures to live by values of love, peace, generosity, and self-control, which rather than being killjoy and life-denying are life-affirming.

According to St Paul this is the path God took himself in Jesus Christ. He argued in his letter to the Philippians that God took the 'form of a slave' by being born in human likeness and then through his obedience to death on a cross brought about the universal liberation of all humankind – the 'glorious liberty of the children of God' as he calls it in Romans.

Let me use a favourite analogy; that of the creative artist, the painter with a canvas stretched across a frame and a palette of paints. You are the artist. Your creativity is your driving instinct for God, which you might call your faith. Your canvas and frame is the Bible and the Church and your paints your moral response. Each of us who is searching for a relationship with God must paint our own picture and each painting will be different. In the pictures that we eventually display in our art gallery there will be evidence of immense technical skill and mastery of colour; there will also be great imagination and creativity, and a lot of rule breaking and experimentation in the pursuit of truth.

Denominations and Church divisions

The reality of the modern Church is that it is fragmented into hundreds of denominations and shades of opinion and most of the large Churches – Roman Catholic, Baptist, Anglican, Orthodox – are umbrella organisations for a wide variety of belief and practice. Typical differences are over Biblical interpretation, moral understanding, styles of worship (traditional or modern), leadership and authority (women priests?), engagement with society or retreat from 'the world'. Churches have wasted an enormous amount of energy and time arguing about these issues to the detriment of their credibility in society. We have seemed to be obsessed with introspective, churchy agendas that have no relevance to the 21st century – sort of fiddling while Rome burns. Still the Anglican Church is consumed with arguments about homosexuality and whether women should become bishops. I don't want to add another divisive voice but I do want to stand up for and affirm the tradition of freedom and criticism in religion, not only because I believe it is right, but because I think it can open the doors of Christian faith to many more people. The points I make are not unique to the liberal tradition and whenever one gets into conversation with people from other traditions you find that there are many areas of overlap and mutuality, and also many areas of misunderstanding that could easily be clarified. But we are by nature protective of our own positions and tend to exaggerate differences in the process of self-identity.

Letter from a student

I received this letter from a student, which expresses at first hand what I am trying to say. It refers to my church in Oxford, but there didn't seem much point in disguising the fact.

'I started going to St Mary's nearly three years ago. At that time I was looking for an open and questioning approach to Christianity. I needed a supportive environment in which to explore the uncertainties of my faith. I felt unhappy and confused because my Christian life and beliefs seemed to have little to do with my experience of ordinary life and contemporary events.

While 'doing the rounds' of the Oxford Churches I decided to go to the Sunday Parish Eucharist at the University Church. I was surprised! Despite the formal title and imposing architecture, I felt at home. The service left me spiritually uplifted, the sermon resonated with my everyday experience and above all I felt that my faith in Jesus Christ needed further exploration.

St Mary's has given me the room to be myself and to explore my doubts and fears. Above all, I have been challenged to accept that I am loved by God and, in return, to love not only God, but my neighbours and even my enemies as well.

I don't want to belong to a church that tells me they have all the answers, because God is bigger than any of us and I believe we ought to live out the Gospel by exploring our faith, by loving others, by prayer, and by a commitment to social action.'

A summary of liberal Christianity

As a launch pad for what follows, I offer this summary of liberal Christianity. Inevitably it's a personal view and there are those who would disagree. But whether they do or not this is what I believe.

Liberal Christianity is biblical, open, liturgically conservative, traditional, ethical, public, and concerned with Christian action.

Biblical

Liberals value Scripture as much as anyone because it is the foundation of faith. It reveals the nature of God and tells the story of salvation. Like all tradition Scripture requires critical appraisal and we try to read the Bible creatively and critically.

Open

Liberals believe that Christian discipleship and theological understanding is an ongoing, developing process and they therefore expect theological ideas to be questioned in the same way as other knowledge claims are questioned. They believe that faith is enriched when Christianity is in dialogue with other disciplines such as science and literature.

Liberals tend to be inclusive rather than exclusive. That is, they try not to hold a narrow view of what it is to be Christian and to be open to people who approach Christianity from unconventional or uncertain positions.

Liberals celebrate the pluralism and diversity of human culture for all the variety and colour it offers. They don't want everyone to be the same and they see the importance of honouring and respecting people of other faiths and of no faith. This is not to diminish or water down Christianity – they affirm their Christian faith proudly – but it is humbly to acknowledge the variety of God's creation.

Liturgically conservative
Perhaps because liberal theology is often exploratory and risk-taking, liberals at worship like something familiar and secure. In Anglicanism liberals tend to go for the traditional eucharistic liturgy shared with the Roman Catholic Church. This gives a sense of historic continuity and also a sense of belonging to a wide Church. Those who make significant links between theology and the creative arts naturally prefer beautiful worship.

Ethics
The liberal moral view is sometimes caricatured as one in which 'anything goes'. In fact liberals have a high sense of morality based on the teaching of Jesus. His (God's) self-giving love is seen as a model for all moral action. Jesus did not create a moral code with provision for all situations, but he did give a clear principle for making moral decisions, namely – what would be the most selflessly loving action in any particular circumstances?

Jesus' own ethics were essentially humane, exemplified in Sabbath healing and bringing dignity to people who were despised in a hypocritical and judgmental society – for example, the tax gatherer, the gentile woman, the woman who anointed his feet. This is the model that persuades liberals to try to be compassionate and humane in moral matters.

Public
While Christian tradition sets up an opposition between the 'church' and the 'world' and the 'spirit' and the 'flesh', the liberal emphasis is on the incarnation,

on the Word becoming flesh. This means that Christian theology should take its agenda from the world and should engage with the public issues of the day. Christianity belongs not just in the churches, but in the market place, the media, parliaments, and in the streets. Christianity must by definition avoid being segregated or self-protectively introspective.

Christian action

The liberal slogan for evangelism would be St Francis of Assisi's instruction to his Brothers, 'Preach the Gospel everywhere, if necessary using words'. Christian action should be the natural by-product of Christian faith and Christianity's greatest advertisement.

So it's all questions and no answers?

Here are some answers:

- God exists
- Jesus Christ was a historical figure who revealed the nature of God
- The Bible is our principle source of Christian Faith
- The Church's tradition has crystallised many of the basic issues of faith
- Many people are persuaded to believe because of their religious experience
- Faith presents us with moral imperatives, ideals and standards
- There is a tension between faith and reason
- To question a belief is not to dismiss it but to refine it
- I believe in the reality of God, but often wonder where God is in a particular situation, especially in suffering and evil.

2.
The Word of the Lord?

It would be impossible to write a book about Christianity without frequent references to the Bible because it contains all the basics of what Christians believe.

Although it usually appears as a single volume between two covers it is in fact a collection of documents written by different authors over a very long period of time and is understood by Christians to give an account of the revelation of God through two thousand years of Jewish history, culminating in the New Testament story of Jesus Christ. There is scarcely any evidence of the historical Jesus outside the New Testament, so it is a totally indispensable document.

In the life of the Church some Christians emphasise the importance of the Bible more than others, even to the extent of certain groups identifying themselves as 'bible-believing' Christians. This usually means that they believe the Bible contains God's actual words and intentions vouchsafed to the individual writers. Of course the very use of the term 'bible-believing' implies that there are other people claiming to be Christians who don't believe the Bible, or at least don't believe it adequately or in the correct way.

I probably come into that category of insufficient faith. But I have to say that as a liberal Christian my faith relies on the Bible just as much as anyone else's. I claim it as absolutely central to my Christianity, although of one thing there is no doubt, I don't read it in quite the same way as the self-styled 'bible believers', or indeed in the same way as many less extreme, but nevertheless literal-minded Christians.

Liberals accept the authority of the Bible for themselves and for the Church they belong to and I want to explore and unpack the basis of that authority.

I find God's character intensely revealed in much of the text but regard the words as being unequivocally those of the men and women who wrote them.

The important thing to me is that these words record the response of people who witnessed the events, particularly the life of Jesus, in which God's action and character was revealed. The revelation is located not primarily in the text but in the events behind it, and in that sense one can say that the Bible is the inspired Word of God. It is inspirational in a particularly spiritual way. It conveys truth about God's love and commitment to the world and it often conveys this truth in figurative ways, just as Shakespeare conveys truth about jealousy, the 'green-ey'd monster', in his play about Othello's distrust of his young wife.

I say that I find 'much' of the text revealing. This means I freely admit I don't consider the entire Bible revelatory or inspirational. Sometimes when I read a particularly dull passage of Jewish history, or a bloodthirsty passage from the Psalms, I want to say 'This is definitely *not* the word of the Lord'. And that doesn't apply just to the Old Testament. For instance, the story in Matthew of Jesus paying his taxes with a coin found miraculously in a fish's mouth is so out of character with the rest of the portrait of Jesus (in the temptation in the wilderness he absolutely refuses to use his godly power to his own advantage by turning stones to bread or jumping from the pinnacle of the Temple) that I refuse to say, 'This is the Gospel of Christ' when it is read in church. And what can be divinely inspired about the lists of Jesus' ancestors in Matthew and Luke (especially since they disagree with each other) or St Paul saying that it is shameful for women to speak in church?

But I know this attitude will be regarded as heresy by a very large number of people, including some in my own congregation who are used to a very free thinking approach to theology. The problem is that there is a literalist streak in most of us that teases us with the question: if you say you don't believe *all* of the Bible, how can you trust *any* of it to be true? You can't pick and choose: you can't take the bits that suit you and discard the bits that don't, otherwise the Bible would have no authority. If, for example, you say that you don't accept the virgin birth – that Jesus was miraculously conceived, as Matthew and Luke suggest he was – then why should you accept anything else that their gospels tell you?

My reply would be that the revelation in 'Holy Scripture' is located in the broad sweep of the narrative, not in minute detail. We are able to deduce the character of God from the scriptures, get an impression, an overall picture, which we have to view by standing back from the minutiae of the text, just as you stand back from a portrait to see what the artist intends. An English professor friend of mine once said that mystery is something to be explored, not defined. And that also applies to God. We often speak of God as a mystery, as

Cowper's famous hymn puts it, 'God moves in a mysterious way, his wonders to perform', and since God is always considered to be infinitely greater than the human mind can grasp, that mystery will always defy definition.

We also have to recognise that many of the stories of the Bible are symbolic in meaning and not necessarily factual in the modern historical sense. The miracle of Water into Wine is a good example of what I mean. Whatever actually happened at the wedding reception that day in Cana of Galilee is secondary to the spiritual message that God's glory is visible in Jesus, and that the difference between the new religion he proclaims and the old religion is like the difference between wine and water. Also the story suggests that he turned an extraordinarily large amount of water into wine – twelve pitchers (probably intended to represent the twelve tribes of Israel) each containing several gallons – far more than the guests could have drunk!

It also strikes me as very significant that Jesus himself did much of his teaching by telling parables, which were clearly not intended to be taken literally but to make theological points in a figurative way. Their titles are some of the most famous phrases of the Bible: The Good Samaritan, the Prodigal Son, the Wise and Foolish Virgins, The Sower. These are illustrative stories that don't just have just one meaning, but several layers of meaning. There is no correct interpretation, but each parable is intended to provoke the hearers to think for themselves. No language can be totally literal anyway. We use metaphors all the time and Jesus used metaphors. The Kingdom of God is like a mustard seed; faith is like a pearl of great price; the gospel message is corn to be thrown generously over good and stony ground alike.

So what is the status of the Bible for the liberal Christian? I would say three things:

1. The Bible can be said to be the Word of God in the sense that it provides words *about* God and gives an account of the life of Jesus, the 'Word made flesh', based on the testimony of those who knew him.
2. It is religious writing that has been marked out as foundational for the Christian faith, but, like all tradition, it requires critical appraisal. This critical appraisal will seek to answer such questions as who wrote the various books and when? What was each writer's aim? To what extent was the writer recording traditions that had developed by word of mouth over a long period? How did the historical circumstances of the time influence the particular editorial angle that the writer puts on his account? For example it is thought that St Matthew wrote his Gospel for a Jewish Christian audience

and that Luke wrote his for a gentile Christian audience. How do the social and intellectual changes that have occurred in the past two thousand years influence our interpretation of what is written?

Questions like these are not radical or new, but have formed the basis for biblical studies in theological colleges and universities for a hundred and fifty years. Every clergyperson will have thought about them and the very great majority will have found their Christian understanding enhanced and enriched by doing so. It's rather like discovering that the more you understand the complexities of football or cricket the more you enjoy the game. Or the more you are able to analyse a piece of music, whether classical or pop, the more you are able to appreciate it.

3. Thirdly, it is important to see that although the Bible is the foundation document for Christian faith, it doesn't give an answer to all possible moral dilemmas or all possible theological questions. It simply addresses the theological and moral issues that cropped up in the life and times it describes. In our desire however to find biblical authority for the particular view we hold, it can be tempting to take a single verse out of context and try to prove a case from it. For example, the Book of Leviticus, which is one of the law books of the Jewish Scriptures, contains laws that were developed by a nomadic society of the Middle East in the seventh century BC. That doesn't mean that its teachings are wrong, but that at least we should recognise their context. One verse in particular has been taken as the principal biblical evidence against homosexuality. Leviticus 18:22 says that homosexuality is an abomination. This issue hits the headlines periodically and last time it was in the news a satirical email was circulated that pointed out that Leviticus also says eating shellfish is an abomination. And that anyone with a defect in their sight may not approach the altar of God, so what about people who wear reading glasses? Or since touching the skin of a dead pig makes a person unclean, does this mean I cannot play football?

So I repeat that revelation in 'Holy Scripture' is located in the broad sweep of the narrative, not in minute detail. To illustrate how this works in practice, let us take a longer look at the issue of the status of women. We know that in the culture of Jesus' time women were treated as inferior to men in terms of religion, marriage, and law. A woman was defined in relation to the principal man of her household, as daughter or wife, as a kind of possession. She could be divorced at her husband's command and stoned for adultery. Writing to the Ephesians and the Corinthians respectively, St Paul said that the husband is the head of the wife just as Christ is the head of the church and that women should be silent in church. Yet, on the other hand, and in apparent contradiction, he tells the Galatians that there is no longer Jew or Greek, slave or free, male and female; 'for all of you are one in Christ Jesus'. If this writing is authoritive for Christians, what should their attitude to women be?

Of course there is other biblical evidence to be adduced. The Book of Genesis says that humankind was made *in the image of God* – an idea that has become foundational in the Christian understanding of humanity. And what can we learn from Jesus? We find that he had some very close women followers: Mary, Martha, Mary Magdalene, Joanna, and Salome are named in the gospels. Some of these were the first witnesses of his resurrection and although they are not given the status of disciples by the gospel writers, they clearly had a role that was as significant in Jesus' ministry. So Jesus seems to have had an attitude to women that was radical for his time and which is well illustrated by two significant events in the gospels. The first is the story of the woman who interrupted an all male supper party to anoint Jesus' feet with expensive ointment and wiped them with her hair. The act was audacious and in the opinion of the other guests scandalous. They said that she was a sinner and how could he allow her to do such an intimate thing. But Jesus replied that she had given him a better welcome than his host, and that because of her great love her sins were forgiven. The second story is of the woman caught in the act of adultery and about to be stoned to death. Her accusers try to trap Jesus by asking what he thinks is the right punishment for her. He replies that the law is right and that whichever of the accusers has no sin should cast the first stone. The consequence is that no one dares make the first move to kill her and he tells her to go and sin no more.

So although there are contradictions in the Bible about the status of women, the broad sweep argues for the equality of the sexes and the view that all human beings have dignity in the sight of God. Also, I would want to give greater weight to the narrative passages that describe Jesus' attitude and teaching than to passages that try to interpret him. That, besides, is what Christianity is always trying to discern – what Christ would do or say in any given situation, because that must be the ultimate authority for Christian action.

Who reads the Bible now?

But there's a basic problem: not so many people read the Bible these days. There are several reasons for this. For a start people generally read less and watch more TV.

This is just one aspect of a cultural revolution that has taken place over the past fifty years and which in Britain, at least, has militated against Christianity. In my childhood in the 1950s every school day began with an act of Christian worship, which included a Bible reading, Sunday was a quiet day with every shop firmly closed and a good attendance at afternoon Sunday school. Even though only nine out of the 28 boys in my class went to church, Christianity was the public religion, and Britain was a country unified by the common purpose of rebuilding after the Second World War. With the 60s and 70s came international jet travel, increased mobility, and immigration and that in turn brought cultural and religious plurality in which religion became increasingly private as we tried to honour each others' traditions. Religious education in schools was no longer biblical and Christian, but comparative, learning about the world faiths. Now readings from the Bible in school are rare.

Over the same period Western First World society has become richer and more materialistic. Sunday, the traditional day of rest, is now a principal shopping day in which 'retail therapy' replaces the re-creative process of contemplating the ultimate purpose of one's life through prayer and reflection. The shopping mall has become the cathedral of the secular culture and the 'Argos' catalogue its bible.

Consequently fewer people read the 'Holy Bible' and very few have much idea of its content. A class of 12-year-olds visited my church in Oxford to learn about its history. It was an extremely disconcerting experience for me because as I began to talk I slowly realised that they didn't have *any* of the vocabulary. They had no notion of altar, pulpit, cross, or font and not one of them could tell me the basic story of Easter or who was killed on Good Friday, even though they all looked forward to their 'Easter holidays'. If they didn't know about Easter, what chance had I got with Pentecost? Even Christmas has lost most of its religious significance with some states and local authorities designating it simply a mid winter festival or 'Winterval', in deference to those of other faiths and none.

So what do I conclude from this? Lack of familiarity with the Bible is simply a cultural reality that makes talking about Christianity more difficult. The Christian apologist can take nothing for granted and enquirers about Christianity almost certainly need to be introduced to the basic story. One of the best ways, I'm sure, is to read Matthew, Mark, or Luke's gospel from start to finish. It doesn't take very long and it gives shape to the story, which can be lost when people hear short Bible readings out of context.

Perhaps also there ought to be a 'reader' or anthology of 'Best Bits from the Bible'. Below I have chosen my personal 'Best Bits'. They are based purely on preference, as passages that I know and love, rather than systematically – although, as I said at the beginning, the Bible isn't a systematic book with a single strand of argument, but a collection of religious history, theology, and poetry. I hope that for anyone who hasn't read the Bible for a long time these suggestions will provide a good taster.

My best Old Testament bits

The story of creation	Genesis 1-2:3
Jacob dreams of a ladder between heaven and earth	Genesis 28:10-19
Jacob wrestles with God on the river Jabbok	Genesis 32:21-30
Moses meets God in the burning bush	Exodus 3 and 4
The Ten Commandments	Exodus 20:1-17
David, Bathsheba and Nathan the prophet	2 Sam 11-12:9
Solomon and the two women	1 Kings 3:16-28
God speaks to Job from the whirlwind	Job 38
The inescapability of God	Psalm 139
Remember now thy creator	Ecclesiastes 12
Arise my love	Song of Solomon 2
The comfort of the Lord	Isaiah 40
The suffering servant	Isaiah 53
Valley of the dry bones	Ezekiel 37
A cry for social justice	Amos 1-5

My best New Testament bits

In the beginning was the Word	John 1:1-14
Christmas	Luke 2
Jesus sets out his manifesto	Luke 4:16-24
The Sermon on the Mount	Matthew 5-7
The Beatitudes	
You are the salt of the earth	
Solomon in all his glory	
The Good Samaritan	Luke 10: 25-37
The Prodigal Son	Luke 15:11-32
The raising of Jairus' daughter	Luke 8:41-56
The woman taken in adultery	John 8:1-11
The Crucifixion	Mark 14-15
Mary in the garden	John 20:1-18
The Road to Emmaus	Luke 24:13-32

Glorious Liberty	Romans 8
Let love be genuine	Romans 12: 9-21
Christian Love	1 Corinthians 13
The Armour of God	Ephesians 6:10-17
Rejoice in the Lord always	Philippians 4
The faith of the Patriarchs	Hebrews 11:8-12 and 32-end
All Things New	Revelation 21:1-6

Top Ten

The Creation	Genesis 1-2
Psalm 139	
Isaiah 40	
Christmas	Luke 2
Sermon on the Mount	Matthew 5-7
Good Samaritan	Luke 10:25-37
Passion Story	Mark 14-15
The Road to Emmaus	Luke 24:13-32
The qualities of Christian love	1 Corinthians 13
The whole armour of God	Ephesians 6:10-17

3.
A hunger for God

The Bible begins with the confident statement that God created the Heavens and the earth. Many people have a hunch that that is true, but not in the way the Bible describes. Astro-physicists now claim that the universe began with a 'Big Bang' 15 billion years and that our planet Earth is 4.55 billion years old. This is an immense length of time and what the Bible sees as the creation is a very small part of it. If we think of the age of the universe as a single hour then intelligent life has only existed for a few seconds and ideas of God for just a fraction of a second.

During that fraction of a second God's public stock has gone up and down, from Christianity's rise in the West to Nietzsche's claim that 'God is dead'. Yet despite the arrogant self-confidence induced by science and technology, and the disillusionment with the idea of moral progress caused by the terrible wars of the 20th century, 90% of the people of the United States of America and 67% of the British population say that they believe in God, although a much smaller number, especially in Britain, actually belong to a church or faith community.

So what do people mean when they say they believe in God? A typical answer would be along the lines that God is creator, or divine goodness, love, justice or truth. These are values that many people admire and aspire to and believe can bring meaning and purpose to life. It is the natural human craving for meaning and purpose that motivates the search for God – the hunger for something ultimately worthwhile and of eternal value amid the all the vicissitudes of life. There's also a sense that love, goodness, and truth are fundamentally *creative* qualities. Christianity certainly recognises that creation is not something that happened once and for all billions of years ago, but is an ongoing process. We share in God's work of creation through the procreation of children, through art, music and literature, and whenever we build up a relationship through love, kindness, and self-giving. Making relationships is the most energisingly creative experience in the whole range of human activity and a key to happiness.

But those who say they believe in God are almost certainly saying more than that there are values they admire and aspire to. There is also a belief that those values exist in some sense beyond us, that they have a reality independent of our imperfect and untidy lives. It is as if there's a celestial store of goodness that we can draw on like plugging into an electricity supply if we choose to do so. It's a view very like that of the Greek philosopher Plato, who believed in a realm of pure ideas or forms 'out there' and that things here on earth owe their existence to it. When I worked in North London lots of young parents, who never ordinarily came to church, brought their children to be baptised because, as they explained, they wanted them to learn how to live a Christian life and to 'choose for themselves when they grow up'. By Christian life they meant a morally good life, a life of decent citizenship, that hopefully would make them both pleasant and successful. Such an attitude is a half way house on the journey to belief in God. It is belief in, as you might say, the *Good* rather than in God.

When I first worked in London my vicar wrote a play called 'The Trial of Job' which we performed in St Paul's Cathedral. Job was a pious and wealthy Jew who had his faith tested by bankruptcy, pustular skin diseases, and so called 'comforters' who insisted that his extreme suffering must have been brought about by extreme evil on his part – which wasn't true. In the play Job had thousands of words to learn.

'I have written this part for you,' said my vicar, seeking to flatter.

'And how about you?' I asked.

'I,' said the vicar. 'I will play God' – which he did, reading his script from the pulpit of St Paul's and dressed in the uniform worn by Lord Raglan in the film 'The Charge of the Light Brigade', which had recently been a hit in West End cinemas. He was a sort of hybrid of Mussolini, the English Aristocracy, and God. I was dressed in a threadbare suit, like a city clerk.

Of course God had wonderful lines. The Bible says that his voice came out of a whirlwind. 'Job, where were you when I laid the foundation of the earth? Tell me, if you have understanding … Can you bind the chains of the Pleiades, or loose Orion's belt? Can you draw out Leviathan with a fishhook, or press down its tongue with a cord?'

Job was simply overwhelmed by the awesome majesty and power of God. It was not just the macho image of a superhuman angler with the great sea monster on the end of his line, but God's infinitely creative power and sheer inventive genius – 'Were you there when I laid the foundation of the earth? Who laid

its cornerstone when the morning stars sang together and all the heavenly beings shouted for joy?' Hearing this poetry Job had no alternative but to repent.
His life takes a new direction and he comes not to resent his trials but to look at
life through God's eyes.

Eventually the play was performed by the BBC with professional actors and
I remember my vicar's dismay when the accounts department said they would
only pay him half the author's fee because half the words were taken direct from
the Bible. But the point I want to make is that the vicar, dressed as Lord Raglan, summed up for me in a humorous way the transcendence of God – God's
otherness, the greatness and the power and the glory. When I think about God
I think instinctively of this aspect first, which actually I find awesome and fear
inducing and a far cry from any tame, suburban God who is concerned with
good manners and good citizenship. What's the point of having a God if that
God doesn't stretch beyond everything that we know and understand and make
demands beyond what we are initially prepared to give? God must be God!

Of course I don't argue that my instinct for God is superior to anyone else's
and I think that the 90% and 67% who claim to believe in God are also expressing a natural hunger for transcendence. But how is that hunger to be satisfied?
The problem with transcendence is that it is, almost by definition, inaccessible.
Somehow what is invisibly distant and 'out there' needs to be made concrete in
our present experience. We can often find truth and quality of life elusive, just
out of reach, just beyond us and we need to find ways of getting in touch. For
some people this is achieved by listening to live music, reading, or walking in
beautiful countryside, or by watching films or going to the theatre. Besides, the
job of artists and writers is to make revelations and to show us things about
reality that we hadn't previously seen for ourselves and bring them closer. But
maybe even here I am assuming too much – art tends to be a minority interest
and some aspects of it expensive and elitist.

As I write, two stories prominent in the British press are the fifth anniversary
of the death of Diana, Princess of Wales and the remembrance of two 10-year-
old girls murdered in the Cambridgeshire village of Soham. The churchyard in
Soham, which is no mean plot of land, has been filled with flowers. In the week
following the death of Diana the public spent 25 million pounds on flowers
to lay at her shrines, compared with an average annual expenditure at florists
in Britain of 35 million pounds. Why should so many thousands of people lay
flowers, send messages and join in the mourning when *they didn't know them*?
Isn't this evidence of mass spiritual searching? These were events that evoked
sympathy and self-identity – Diana had famously suffered, she was young

and beautiful and her death was dramatic; the murder of the Soham girls was shocking and perverted and the grief of their parents, dignified and noble, was evident to everyone. They were events that changed the public mood, pulled people up in their tracks, and forced a kind of religious question, what are we here for and what is life about? The ritual of laying flowers in vast numbers either outside Buckingham Palace or in Soham churchyard was a way of seeking a language in which to express spiritual hunger, however raw or unformed. What can I say? What can I do? People recognise the need for expiation, repentance, forgiveness and hope; how do we learn from this; how can we do better in the future? How can we centre our minds on the things the really matter in life?

Those who wrote the Bible were aware of the need for a language to express this raw spiritual need and it tells a story that in itself is a kind of language of God. The important thing about God in the Bible is that he is seen as personal, not a god of ideas alone, but a God who enters relationship with people and influences their lives. It is the main theme of the Old Testament, which describes the developing relationship between God and his chosen people. This relationship is a pledge of commitment between the people of Israel and God, in which they promise loyalty and worship in return for protection and divine leadership. But the Old Testament God is only halfway personal. This is a God who appears on mountain tops, who speaks from clouds or in dreams, who is like a king, a judge, or a shepherd, who can be intensely present in holy places, but in the end is always awesome and a bit frightening. If God is to be truly personal he has to be expressed in a far more intimate way than a voice in a whirlwind.

This is where the New Testament takes over, beginning with the story of Bethlehem and Christmas. God becomes man. The eternal creator enters human history in the form of Jesus of Nazareth, a first-century Jew living in Palestine, who is the subject of the next chapter.

But there is another idea of God that I find helpful and which I'd like to mention first, suggested by St Paul when he addressed the philosophers in Athens. He had gone to the Areopagus, where the Athenians met for discussion and debate, and he gave a speech that was not only clever but also shows how the search for God in the ancient mind was similar to our own. He said that walking through the city he had noticed how extremely religious they were. For example, he had seen an altar dedicated to 'an unknown god.' He then proceeded to argue that the unknown God they were seeking was none other than the creator God revealed in Jesus Christ. He said that although people grope to find God, God is not far away, for 'in him we live and move and have our being'.

The idea of God as a sustaining personal environment in whom we can live and move and have our being, rather than an external source of goodness and creative power that has to be tapped in to, has definite attractions. It provides a more unified view of the relationship between God and humankind, but it does raise the obvious difficulty that, if we think of God as a kind of medium for life, as water is the medium for fish, why some people aspire to spirituality and others don't. If everyone breathed in God as they breathe in oxygen, then presumably they would all be influenced by godly qualities. But that is transparently not the case, so I take it as a helpful additional metaphor for an understanding of God. It's a very similar idea to Paul's when he speaks of Christians having a life *in* Christ. He tells the Christians in Rome (Romans 6:11) that they must consider themselves 'dead to sin and alive to God in Christ Jesus'. In a way to be *in* Christ is obviously a metaphor, but he does have a more concrete view of Christ as a spiritual entity and as the body of people who make up the Church. When he speaks of Christ in this context he is not thinking of the physical person of Jesus of Nazareth, but of the resurrected and ascended Christ; a Christ who takes on a much more transcendent and mystical nature, somehow unlimited in heaven rather than limited on earth. So to be in Christ, or to live and move and have your being in God, is an incorporative image, more an image of belonging and interdependence than one of being a medium for survival such as water or air. In fact Paul says that Christians make up the body of Christ on earth – a body that has 'many members', limbs and organs, which must work together in harmony for the body to function effectively.

4.

Love came down at Christmas

The hunger for God must be satisfied. It is one thing to have a hunch that God exists but quite another to be persuaded that that hunch could present a challenge to your life. You need to know more and Christmas begins the process because it is the opening chapter in the life of Christ.

Christmas is found in only two of the four gospels. Matthew has the Wise men with their gifts of gold, frankincense and myrrh; King Herod, the massacre of the innocents, and the holy family's escape into Egypt. Luke has the shepherds, the angels, no room in the inn, and the baby lying in a manger. Both make it clear that there is something uniquely important about Mary's son. Luke says that he will be great, and will be called the Son of the Most High, and Matthew says that he is the fulfilment of an Old Testament prophecy that a virgin shall conceive and bear a son, who will be called Emmanuel, which means, God is with us.

This idea of God with us, that God enters the world of human experience, is the essence of Christmas and the theme of many Christmas Carols. *Once in Royal David's City* says that Jesus 'came down to earth from heaven'. *Hark the Herald Angels Sing* refers to Jesus as the 'heaven-born Prince of peace'. Other carols mention the 'heavenly babe', the boy who is 'king of all creation', and *O little town of Bethlehem* says that 'God imparts to human hearts the blessings of his heaven'.

Is this the 'magic' of Christmas? That may not be a very theological way of putting it, but you often hear people say that there is something 'magical' about Christmas and I am fascinated to know what the secret ingredient is. Why are Christmas Carol Services far and away the most popular church services of the year? People flock to them and many churches have to issue tickets because they can't accommodate the numbers who want to attend. Schools, shops, charities and Lord Mayors like to hold their own services. Is it a hunger for God or is it merely that they get us in the mood for Christmas and get the spiritual bit out of the way so we are free to enjoy the self-indulgence that follows? It's hard to put your finger on it.

For those of us who live in the Northern Hemisphere where Christmas comes in the darkest days of the year, there is great poignancy in the celebration of light. It is no accident that Jesus has been called 'the light of the world', and that one of the popular prophetic texts, read at carol services, from Isaiah, says that 'the people who walked in darkness have seen a great light'. The same image is used at the beginning of John's Gospel, in the passage usually read at the end of carol services, where John says of Christ that, 'the true light, which enlightens everyone, was coming into the world'. Anyone who has watched a small child gaze with wonder at the twinkling lights on a Christmas tree will understand a little of what is meant by the 'magic' of Christmas. That is not just sentimentality; the fascination with light in darkness is an adult thing too. It symbolises hope and promise of new opportunity and growth. Darkness is the symbol of incarceration and death; light is the symbol of freedom and life. Add to this the story of a homeless mother giving birth to a baby in a stable, and exotic Eastern potentates being led by a star to worship the child, and you have more 'magic'. Even that doesn't really explain why Christmas is the most spiritually evocative part of the Christian story in contemporary culture. There must be something more. It seems to me that the story of the birth of Jesus bridges a gap between the ordinariness and occasional disappointments of human experience and the world of God's perfection. The instinctive response when contemplating divine perfection is to ask how this can possibly connect with what I experience and see around me, rather as the ordinary person wonders how their life could possibly connect with the life of royalty or Hollywood stars. This was a theme cleverly explored in the film *Notting Hill*. Christmas implies that although God might seem abstract and 'out there', in fact godliness *can* touch our lives. And as the carols point out, the 'maker of the stars and skies', the divine super-power, enters the world of human experience, not as a prince wrapped in silk, but into the lowly cattle shed where he is laid in straw. This is massively persuasive. We are accustomed to privilege and hierarchy, fuelled by the tabloid press, to the kitschily named infants of footballers and pop stars baptised in country hotels behind a barricade of exclusive deals with 'Hello' magazine. But when God is presented as a humble outsider for whom there is no room in the inn, the penny drops and we recognise godliness in the unexpected. The very surprise of it all – the inversion of the values one has come to expect, the values of self-seeking human nature – adds credibility to the whole story. God is for everyone, not just the privileged few. As Jesus would later say, 'those who want to save their life will lose it, and those who lose their life for my sake, and for the sake of the gospel, will save it. For what will it profit them to gain the whole world and forfeit their life?' [Mark 8:35] and as Mary sang in the Magnificat, when she first learnt that she was pregnant, 'he has exalted the humble and meek'. These are telling signs of God with us.

The 'magic' of Christmas might seem to be a cliché, but one of the reasons why the Festival has large-scale appeal is that it undermines clichés. It forces us to look at the world from God's point of view instead of our own and we may not like what we see. Again the carols spell out the message: 'now the holly bears a berry as green as the grass, and Mary bore Jesus who dies on the cross'. The joy of birth, heralded by the angels' *Gloria in Excelsis* is tainted with portents of suffering and death. This is our experience too. You can't live in the world for long without learning that the wonderful gift of life carries with it a high risk of suffering. The suffering, at best, makes us aware of the preciousness of life, and when life is valued in that way people see the need to love their enemies and to fight against the divisions of rank, gender, race, religion and national allegiance that so ravage the human race.

I hope that in trying to understand the appeal of Christmas I am not just superimposing my own ideas on it. It's ironic that if God *is* recognised in the inversion of accepted values this festival, based on a story of poverty, humility and goodwill, should have turned into a commercial frenzy of buying and greed. One Christmas I made a poster featuring the words, 'Glory to God in the Highest', and some joker erased the 'e' in highest so that it read 'Glory to God in the High St'. It can be very annoying when posters are defaced, but this one worked rather well. If the values of God are glorified in the High Street, they should stand as a prophetic reproach of what we do there, especially at Christmas.

The idea of 'God with us' is what Christianity calls the 'Incarnation' – the embodiment of God in human form. The beginning of St John's Gospel puts it quite unequivocally, 'the Word became flesh and lived among us', and St Paul accepted the same theological idea when he explained to the Colossians that 'in him (Jesus Christ) all the fullness of God was pleased to dwell'.

Despite the popular appeal of Christmas, the idea that God enters the world in the form of a human being can seem very odd. The obvious objection is that it's difficult to see how Jesus could be both human and divine. If God is an all knowing, all-powerful, timeless being, how could he possibly be contained in one limited human life? It doesn't make a lot of sense and the more you try to explain it, perhaps by arguing that God reduces his 'godness' in order to be human, the sillier it becomes. But the Christians who wrote the creeds in the fourth and fifth centuries thought it was a crucial issue and spent a lot of energy trying to make a watertight case that Jesus was perfect God and perfect man. For example they said that he was of 'one being with the Father'. The reason they thought this so important was that they believed that Jesus could only take away the sins of the world if he was fully God. This is a question that we shall consider later in the chapter 'Jesus Saves'

Actually it is of course impossible to make a watertight case about the nature of God. It's obviously useful to marshal your arguments and to try to think clearly, but no theologian or philosopher has ever been able to prove anything about God and I think it's important to remember that, especially when people, on either side of the discussion, are inclined to be dogmatic. For me the doctrine of the Incarnation is crucial to understanding Christianity, but I'm inclined to a common sense approach which simply says that people recognised in Jesus a special god-revealing quality. This is the angle taken by the gospel stories themselves. They tell of people for whom meeting Jesus is such an overwhelming experience that they find themselves asking each other what kind of person he is. Who is this who can forgive sins? Who is this who can heal the blind and the deaf? Or, when he stilled the storm on the Sea of Galilee, who is this that the winds and the waves obey him? The questions are not answered but the implication clear enough: he is the Messiah, whose arrival the Jews expected to be accompanied by just such events as these. There is no game, set and match proof that Jesus is God, but the circumstances of his life certainly reveal something of what many people identify as godliness. At the climax of Mark's Gospel in the crucifixion story the centurion, who watched Jesus die, says, 'Truly this man was God's Son!' But what led him to this conclusion? It wasn't suddenly revealed to him by philosophical argument – soldiers who crucified people were hard men with built-in emotional immunity, used to being cursed by their desperate victims – but having seen the gracious way in which Jesus faced his execution, the centurion was moved to believe. And that is the key: the recognition of Jesus as the revealer of God is a response of faith. It is a response of faith that can make sense despite the barrage of intellectual objections offered by science and philosophy against the mythology-laden belief system of the ancient world and the historical reliability of the texts – the most familiar of which is the questioning of the virgin birth. Despite these objections the moral character of Jesus has stridden across the pages of Western history and left a mark on our institutions and public life. The high proportion of people who say they believe in God would, I suspect, express that belief in terms of the moral character of Jesus.

For Jesus, too, godliness was a response to faith in the sense that he seemed to draw his godliness from his belief. He lived his whole life in prayerful relationship to God whom he called Father. At the end of his life, in the Garden of Gethsemane, he prayed not to have to suffer torture, but added 'yet, not my will but yours be done.' By calling God Father he wasn't commenting on his genetic origin but, in the best Jewish tradition, accepting the headship of God and affirming his complete obedience to God's will. He no doubt also believed that his relationship with God had a supernatural dimension. He believed that the Kingdom of God was breaking into the temporal order in his own lifetime and that its arrival was connected with his own ministry and physical presence in Palestine. Whatever your take on the life of Jesus (and there are many different views) it inaugurated a tremendous spiritual momentum especially after the crucifixion and resurrection.

I discussed this question recently with a young student who was thinking about being ordained. Having talked about the practicalities of becoming a vicar – the selection process, training, the pay – I asked why he wanted to be ordained – is it a convenient job for a person with an academic bent, or is there some theological imperative driving you? He said it was his faith in Jesus Christ. I explained how I understood Christ, in similar terms to the paragraphs above. Then he told me that, in his opinion, you have got to have faith in the extraordinary. 'I am willing,' he said, 'to accept that once in history God broke all the laws of physics and became man. You have got to put behind you questions that don't get you anywhere, like did the virgin birth happen and concentrate on the extraordinary power of God to transform people's lives. You've got to believe in the extraordinary; there's got to be something different and exciting to make it all worthwhile.'

I felt slightly chastened by the young enthusiast and asked for some examples. What are the modern equivalents of water into wine, the transfiguration, the healing miracles? We both suggested possibilities: the work of Mother Teresa, Christianity's involvement in the end of Apartheid in South Africa, Christian Aid, work with the homeless and work for justice for asylum seekers?

It struck me that the extraordinary events of the gospels were in fact intimate and personal rather than world-shatteringly public. Perhaps the secret of seeing how God can transform lives is to see the extraordinary in the ordinary. I thought of the widow who had asked for the story of the wedding at Cana to be read at her husband's funeral 'because he turned water into wine'; I thought of the many voices from the Christian community pleading for reconciliation and forgiveness in international relations and in the rift between rich and poor;

I thought of small examples of healing, forgiveness and fresh starts in broken relationships. But there was more to what he was saying than that, if I understood correctly. He was saying that the extraordinary *makes demands on one's life*. When we experience or intuit God touching our lives in some incarnational way (whether we are thinking literally or metaphorically) the effect, if it is genuine, will make demands on us to live our lives differently. This is what was driving him towards ordination and it is it the force that drives people generally towards discipleship.

5.
Risen today

Why is the resurrection important?

We have considered the hunger for God and how this can be met by the life and teaching of Jesus. Now we need to consider the most extraordinary claim of Christianity – the belief that after his crucifixion and burial, Jesus rose from the dead, and as the living Christ energised the life of the Church. The resurrection is important because it is evidence that God's intervention in the world was effective. It affirms the sovereignty of God by proclaiming the triumph of good over evil and shows that Jesus' work is not defeated by the crucifixion, but strengthened in such a way as to provide hope to his followers and confidence in the future.

That is what it means to Christians, but inevitably people want to ask about the nature of the event: what actually happened? Are we expected to take it literally or symbolically and is the quality of our faith determined by how we answer that question?

As one who is not drawn to the kind of religion that asks you to believe six impossible things before breakfast, I am always immensely encouraged by the accounts of the resurrection in the New Testament. The earliest of these comes in Paul's letter to the Corinthians where he describes various appearances of the risen Jesus to the disciples, culminating in a visionary appearance to himself on the Damascus Road, which changed him from chief persecutor to principle champion of Christianity. These incidents imply that the experience of the risen Christ was spiritual rather than physical, which Paul actually argued for quite specifically in 1 Corinthians 15, where he said that when a person is buried their body 'is sown a physical body, and raised a spiritual body'.

This view is borne out to a certain degree by the later gospels. When Mary

Magdalene meets Jesus in the garden, she doesn't immediately recognise him and thinks he is the gardener. On the road to Emmaus, the disciples who walk with him all day don't recognise him until he breaks bread with them at the evening meal. And when he appears to the disciples in a locked room, he appears and disappears like a vision. On the other hand, of course, there is a strong tradition that argues for his physical resurrection, especially the tradition of the empty tomb and the story of 'doubting Thomas' in which Thomas is asked to prove the resurrection for himself by touching the wounds of Jesus.

However you interpret the resurrection, it is clear from the New Testament and from subsequent Christian reflection that it is not about resuscitation but about the mysterious ongoing life of Christ. You might equally say that it is about the irrepressible life of God and the experience of the Holy Spirit in the world. The language and writing about it is neither scientific nor philosophical, but religious. As Richard Holloway put it in a recent interview: 'If people could really understand that the nature of religion is this wonderful mythic, symbolic, poetic system that's about *deep truth*, then they would relax'.

I think this blurring of the boundaries between historical fact and spiritual revelation is well illustrated by the case of the Turin Shroud. In Turin Cathedral there is a linen cloth alleged to be the shroud used to wrap Jesus for his burial. It has markings on it resembling a man's face, which are said to have been caused by the force of Jesus' physical resurrection. On various occasions scientists have tried to test its authenticity by carbon dating techniques but the best they come up with is that it's a medieval forgery. But just suppose that it had been proved as the genuine shroud of Jesus, providing proof of the resurrection, what difference would that make to the number of people becoming Christians, or to the degree of commitment amongst Christians? I would dare to suggest that it would make next to no difference. What actually happened on that first Easter morning is comparatively unimportant beside the surge of enthusiasm and admiration that grew up around the memory of Jesus. What makes people want to become Christians is not miraculous events but an irresistible admiration for Jesus' teachings and example. The big issue at Easter is not the resurrection but the crucifixion – the fact that this good and innocent man, the Son of God, was deserted by his followers and died so graciously. The resurrection hope that followed was the inevitable consequence of this display of self-giving love and it is in that very graciousness that God's presence is perceived.

This is the point made by Mark's Gospel, which originally ended at Chapter 16 verse 8 without any resurrection account. The Good News for Mark was the godly life revealed in Jesus and recognised by Peter at Caesarea Philippi when he said, 'You are the Christ' – a judgement that was justified by Jesus' subsequent dignity in the face of to death. By ending his gospel with the fear of the women who discovered the empty tomb, it is as if Mark were saying, if you haven't got the message in the story so far, you never will.

If Paul and Mark play down the *spectacle* of the resurrection, we should be grateful to the other writers for stories of exquisite beauty and rich meaning. The Road to Emmaus and the appearance to Mary Magdalene are amongst the most beautiful in the Bible. But none of them, it seems to me, make wild claims or try to convince us against our better judgement with miraculous pyrotechnics – with the possible exception of 'Doubting Thomas'. The resurrection was rooted in ordinary experiences such as fishing, a barbecue on the beach, and breaking bread at Emmaus. It is really no different from today: Christians still have a sense of Christ's presence in relationship and the eucharistic breaking of bread and sharing of wine.

The resurrection must have the crucifixion

In Britain the spring holiday for schools and business is still called the 'Easter' holiday, although the majority, I think, would be pushed to explain what Easter is about in religious terms. Good Friday, which is part of the Easter weekend and the day that marks the death of Christ, is now a day of shopping and sporting events, and although the Easter Day services are well attended, those in Holy Week are very thin. The consequence is that even regular worshippers can miss out on the suffering of Jesus and only get the triumphal bits. The danger of this is that it can lead to the kitsch interpretation of Easter so beloved of commerce: chocolate eggs, Easter bunnies and flowery bonnets.

By contrast this year I spent Good Friday in Granada, in Spain. In the evening we went out to watch the Good Friday processions. Six or seven different churches processed through the streets displaying their effigies of the crucified Christ and the weeping Madonna, bedecked with cascades of lilies and candles. It was a warm night and a carnival atmosphere filled the city – people selling balloons and chestnuts, trinkets and candy. Yet out of respect for the season the shops had been closed on Holy Thursday as well as Good Friday. The pavements were packed with people standing six deep – men, women and children stretching to see the spectacle as it passed by. It was easy pickings for the thief who took my neighbour's purse, passport and credit cards. When the larger than life crucifix came round the corner I was moved to think of the suffering of Christ, the shocking pain and torment of crucifixion. Then the people started to applaud and, thinking this was an old religious custom, I joined in. Were we acknowledging our salvation? Greeting Christ as we might greet the Pope? Then I realised that the float was carried on the backs of about twenty men hidden beneath its skirts. They shuffled along in rhythmic step and *they* were being applauded for the difficulty of their manoeuvre.

People in the crowd flicked away their chestnut shells with casual indifference as one imagined they might in the Colosseum, or having come out to watch the burnings of the Spanish Inquisition.

Leading the processional effigies were numerous 'penitents' – young people so far as one could tell – wearing tall pointy hats, like the Klu Klux Klan, that came right down like masks over their faces. People said the dress was a left over from the Inquisition.

Overall it wasn't a very religious experience, but on the other hand few could have been left in any doubt about the basic story of Good Friday. As I stood on the Granada pavement, I remembered the text from Lamentations: 'Is it nothing to you, all you who pass by? Look and see if there is any sorrow like my sorrow.' That is a key question because it's the one that asks if you care, or if you are moved by the suffering of Jesus. If a person doesn't care, or isn't moved by the self-giving love of Jesus, then the resurrection will mean nothing. How could it? It would be as kitsch as the Easter bunnies. But if one *is* moved by the Passion and does care about it, then the resurrection is the inevitable consequence, because you have been changed and that is the impetus of the new life that the resurrection stories point to.

New beginnings

This theme will be taken up and developed in the chapter 'Jesus Saves', but I want to indulge myself in one more Spanish story. As a family we have taken our Spring holiday for many years in Andalusia. So it isn't surprising that many of my Easter sermons have been illustrated by Spanish experiences.

In the foothills of the Sierra Nevada lies the remote village of Saleres. Its streets are too narrow for cars and the only transport is by donkey. They plod slowly along with their panniers of oranges swaying from side to side. Some of the old women still wash their clothes on the smooth boulders in the river at the bottom of the village. There is an air of almost biblical poverty about the place, with dung in the streets, crumbling walls, and ragged children.

Each year in March (or thereabouts) the young men of the village are allowed to spray graffiti on the walls of the square at the entrance to the honeycomb of narrow streets, and then at Easter the walls are whitewashed clean for the new season. Some of the graffiti is politically angry and some sexually explicit. Writing that stuff on the walls gets it out of the system. It gets it said, out in the open, and then it's all wiped away. It is not the same as sweeping things under the carpet in a kind of escapism, pretending they don't exist, but a way of facing up to the more sinister aspects of human personality such as gratuitous violence and pornography and confronting them.

This is how Easter works. The dark side of human personality and human society comes out in the story of Jesus' death. If you wanted to make a list of the 'graffiti' of the gospel story it wouldn't be difficult. Betrayal for money in the case of Judas, cowardice when Peter said he had never met Jesus, the institutional brutality of ritual execution with soldiers teasing the man they were paid to torture, and the callous indifference of the baying crowd shouting for blood.

These events symbolise human evil and they need, as it were, to be sprayed on a wall in pressurised paint. They need to be out in the open, to leap out like an eyesore, offending passers by. They are shocking and we need to be shocked by them if we are to discover that there is life beyond resentment, injustice, pain, anguish, human failure and knee-jerk reaction.

To push my metaphor even further, I'd say that Jesus' trial, flogging, public humiliation, and crucifixion are God's graffiti sprayed across the world. God is saying, 'I know all about your potential for cruelty, violence, ugliness, hatred, sectarianism, and repression. And I am going to name it in my blood. I am going to get it out into the open. I am going to show that I, God, can also be made to suffer by your sin. But that having absorbed all that you can throw at me, I shall then whitewash the wall of sin and give you a new start.'

6.

Jesus saves

The creeds tell us that Jesus came down from heaven 'for us and for our salvation'. Thus Jesus is the Saviour or the one who saves. But what does this mean? Being saved from what? When I asked a group of students their answers ranged from 'being saved from our sins', to a more Freudian 'being saved from ourselves'. Other suggestions included being saved from evil, death, drug addiction, political oppression, and meaninglessness. Putting these responses together, the group saw their religious faith as having life changing implications at many levels: personal, spiritual, social, political and philosophical.

The Bible answers the question by telling a story – salvation history. It begins with Adam and Eve and culminates with Jesus Christ. Adam and Eve are in paradise until they disobey God's command not to eat the fruit of the Tree of Knowledge. Their disobedience turns them from godlike creatures to mortals, enslaved to sin and death – a condition handed on to their children and successors. In due course, God sent his Son to put matters right and redeem humankind. This redemption was achieved, it was thought, particularly through Jesus' crucifixion. In a famous phrase St Paul says that as in Adam all die, even so in Christ shall all be made alive. The crucifixion happened around the time of the Passover Festival and so it was natural for Jewish Christians, who in Jerusalem were used to the ritual of animal sacrifice in the Temple, to interpret Jesus' death as a kind of sacrifice for sin and to compare it with the sacrifice of a lamb at the Passover Festival.

Early in John's Gospel, when John the Baptist sees Jesus approaching he says, 'Look, here is the Lamb of God who takes away the sins of the world!' It is extraordinary to me that modern Christianity has hung onto this image because the idea that killing an animal or a human being could possibly be a way of removing guilt for wrong doing is offensive and barbaric. However, it is enshrined in our liturgies as in the *Agnus Dei* of the mass; 'O Lamb of God, who takes away the sins of the world' and it's difficult to see how it could be changed.

The crucifixion

Crucifixion was a horrible and cruel way to die – slow, painful, and humiliating. What went through the minds of those who suffered in this way is awful to contemplate. Unable to move your arms and legs, unable to provide for yourself the slightest relief from the flies, the thirst, or the muscle cramps and knowing that all you can do is wait to die is quite unspeakable. So unspeakable in fact that there is very little in literature outside the Bible about it, even though it was a commonplace method of execution. St Paul, however, is not ashamed to refer to it and says at one point, 'we proclaim Christ crucified'. For Paul the crucifixion represented the end of an old order and the beginning of a new and he therefore made it the centrepiece of his preaching. In his first Letter to Timothy he gives a key interpretation of it when he says that Jesus gave his life as a *ransom* for many. The metaphor of a ransom is taken from slavery. A slave could be freed by the payment of a ransom to the owner, rather in the same way as a mortgage is 'redeemed'. When the debt is paid off to the mortgage company they relinquish the hold they have over the property and the house becomes entirely yours.

So is the death of Jesus the debt paid to release humanity from the slavery of sin? Does Jesus die in our place? The New Testament doesn't exactly say this, but the twofold idea that Jesus is the sacrificial Lamb of God and also a 'ransom for many' makes it a hard one to resist and later Christian interpretation has taken it up with gusto. In fact the most popular Christian explanation of how we are saved is the doctrine of 'penal substitution'. According to this theory, which for many conservative Christians is an indispensable fundamental of faith, God's justice requires human sin to be punished by death. But on the other hand because God is merciful he is willing to accept the death of his Son as a substitute. It's a ludicrous scenario by which to portray a loving God because it turns God into a bloodthirsty and capricious tyrant. I also find the theory psychologically flawed. What parent would sacrifice their child? Wouldn't any of us place ourselves, physically if necessary, between our child and any threatening danger? Don't we have an instinctive and occasionally irrational desire to protect our children and promote their welfare? If it's not true to human nature, it's hard to believe that it could be true to divine nature.

I think the notion that salvation is in any way a mechanical process is totally misleading. I guess it grows out the myth that everything in the garden was

lovely until Adam and Eve ate the apple. Once you suggest that their disobedience upset the metaphysical order of things, then to put it right you have a
kind of metaphysical star wars on your hands. You have to think that there is
an imbalance between good and evil somewhere out there in space which can
only be corrected by a specific act or at a specific moment. The three hours that
Christ spent on the cross, or maybe the moment when he died, could be seen
to be that corrective event. But it makes little sense to me to think of the cross
making a difference in the physical or metaphysical order of things. When we
think of salvation are we supposing that God *does* something? Is Jesus *taking
away the sins of the world* in some concrete way, like paying off a debt? Does his
death make a cosmic difference or shift the balance of power between good and
evil? It might be tempting to think in those terms, but my own belief is that God
doesn't need to engage in any kind of Miltonic warfare against evil, or any deals
involving debt and repayment. It is quite sufficient that God is there and that
his nature is to love his creation. What the crucifixion *does* is to reveal the total
commitment of God's self-giving love.

The theologian, Walter Lowe, argues that in modern understanding it is un-
clear whether salvation is an *event that one knows* or *the event of one's knowing*. If
it is the event of one's knowing then it is our response to God that is saving, not
some great metaphysical wheeler dealing in the sky between God's justice and
God's mercy. Just respond to God, connect with God, and you automatically
create the real possibility of living your life on a higher plane.

If you were to ask me what I basically believe about being saved I would reply
that being saved is to do with being in relationship with God, having a sense
of purpose, and looking for a spiritual element in a very materialistic life. As
a Christian I would say that this quality of life is revealed most absolutely in
the life of Jesus Christ, which in itself might be called God's great statement of
commitment to the world. And it is the whole of his life from birth to ascension
that is saving, not just the crucifixion. It seems to me that the events of Christ's
life such as his kindness to the woman taken in adultery, or the words of his
first sermon in the synagogue at Nazareth – 'The Spirit of the Lord is upon me,
because he has anointed me to bring good news to the poor … to proclaim
release to the captives and recovery of sight to the blind, to let the oppressed go
free' – are just as saving as his suffering on the cross. The point is perhaps that
he wouldn't have behaved as he did *in extremis* if he hadn't have behaved with
such grace in all that he did before.

The belief that salvation comes through the whole of the incarnation is fairly
mainstream and not a specifically modern one; it was shared, for example,

by the second-century theologian Irenaeus, who suggested that redemption involves the whole of salvation history from creation, through Easter, to the Second Coming. It is enough to know what God is like through his divine revelation without depending on specific acts of God.

Seeing salvation

In the year 2000 the art critic Neil MacGregor presented a series of programmes for the BBC on Christian religious paintings called 'Seeing Salvation'. The title is taken from the words of Simeon in Luke's Gospel on the occasion of the Presentation of Christ in the Temple. The old man holds the infant Jesus in his arms and says, 'Now mine eyes have seen thy salvation'. The final picture in Neil MacGregor's book is Rembrandt's painting of Simeon holding the Christ child. It is chosen to symbolise the same belief that I have been discussing, that salvation is to be found in the whole Jesus story. It is as visible to Simeon as it is to the centurion at the foot of the cross, who seeing Jesus die says, 'Truly this man was God's Son!'

In the book of the series MacGregor discusses the search for a universal image for the divine and argues that the traditional crucifixion scene lost its impact in the 20th century as the ubiquitous camera captured instant images of world shattering suffering and misery. Crucifixion paintings in any case had not consistently depicted the barbarism of the torture. In some Christ seemed comparatively untroubled and in others he was positively triumphant – the so-called *Christus Rex* depictions. These might be helpful for pious reflection, but were they able to stand beside far worse images: the slaughter of the trenches, the emaciated prisoner in Auschwitz and that famous photograph of a Vietnamese girl walking down the road burning with napalm – a picture that helped to end the Vietnam War? It could equally well be a photograph of the aftermath of a suicide bombing in a Jerusalem café or commuter bus, with all the surrounding carnage.

So MacGregor looks for another image for divinity and cites St Francis of Assisi who claimed that the love felt for a child recalls us most powerfully to our duties of love for all humanity. Hence the pride of place that he gives to Rembrandt's painting. I don't altogether agree with his conclusion because I find divinity revealed much more in Christ the adult, the 'Man for Others' and the 'Suffering Servant' – ideas contained more in Biblical literature perhaps than European painting. I am moved when he washes his disciples feet, and that he appears during his ministry to be homeless, depending on the hospitality of friends. I am thrilled by his radical approach to religion and God – the Sabbath was made for man not man for the Sabbath. But I am sure that MacGregor is right in seeing redemption in much more than the crucifixion. The crucifixion is an important part of it but by no means the whole of it.

Can the cross ever make a difference?

You may think I have made heavy weather of this point and be wondering whether I have seriously undervalued the importance that Christian tradition has given to the cross. If it doesn't actually change the balance of good and evil, what's all the fuss about and how can it help us to deal with contemporary events any differently? The answer is: in the following ways. It is first of all significant, in this world of power politics, that the divine nature is revealed in weakness rather than in strength. If God is willing to suffer the humiliation of the cross, then shouldn't that make us think twice about our egotism, both individual and corporate? Isn't standing by watching the humiliation of nations a bit similar to standing at the cross and mocking, 'If you are the Son of God come down from the cross'?

Secondly, any reading of politics in the light of the cross would have to take into account the fact that the cross is reconciliatory: Jesus said on the cross 'Father, forgive them for they know not what they do'. He did not curse his torturers, although one might think he had every right to do so, but blessed them. Thus he showed that reconciliation is possible at the point when instinct suggests revenge, resentment, and hatred. And it is important in the heat of the political moment to stand back and think of that and ask whether there isn't a better way. In that sense the cross stands in prophetic judgement over the activities and machinations of the world always inviting people to rethink their motivations and the likely consequences of their actions.

Then there is the idea that human suffering is more bearable because God has embraced suffering as part of his being. (I have discussed this in greater detail in the chapter on suffering). When I last had to address this question in a sermon, a young girl, the same age as my daughter, had been killed on her gap year travels in Kenya, possibly by a crocodile. How could the fact of God's suffering on the cross help her family come to terms with their grief? I had to admit that it might not. It was an accident, a silly mistake with a tragic consequence. Her death seemed cruel and so futile that what happened two thousand years ago could scarcely make a difference. Except perhaps to say that however long or short a life is it is valuable to

God. Jesus' life was cut off in its prime and yet he made arguably the greatest impact on history.

This comment came in the same series of addresses that I gave at Easter 2002. I had decided (quite independently of any thought about the work of Neil Macgregor!) to speak on Good Friday about three modern paintings of the crucifixion under the general title 'Portraits of the Passion'. I wanted to think about some aspects of what the crucifixion might mean today. I am not sure that this was particularly about salvation, but more about how the crucifixion can help us to know ourselves – possibly what that student had in mind when she said that being saved meant 'being saved from ourselves'.

On a recent visit to the Vatican Museum in Rome I had noticed a painting of the crucifixion depicting a factory worker in his blue overalls crucified amidst a forest of factory chimneys. I was greatly taken by it, but it was near closing time and we passed on and I haven't been able to trace the picture or the name of the artist since. The picture appealed to me because, although I have never worked in a factory, I identified with it and recognised something of my own history in it. It made the crucifixion seem relevant in a way that frankly surprised me, also by the way arousing an element of nostalgia for my student days in the industrial Northeast of England when I was a young man in the 1960's. I thought of that smoky, dour environment of back-to-back terraced houses, working your fingers to the bone and making ends meet. People spoke of that kind of life with another metaphor from the industrial age, the treadmill, and this very English Christ in his boiler suit was as it were crucified on the treadmill of industrial labour. But the painting could equally well have been a miner at the mineshaft, a slave in the cotton field, a car crash victim at the side of the road, or even the famous photograph of the Vietnamese girl walking down the road burning with napalm.

We need images to identify with that can also function as a catharsis for our suffering. They must also do justice to the appalling things people have to endure, without romanticising or trivialising or glorifying them as often happens in films and video games. That's why I took for my second picture a crucifixion by Picasso. It depicts a chaotic, hellish violence with an agonised Christ figure who seems to be screaming or shouting out. There is a hint of Michaelangelo's Last Judgement with bodies and limbs falling into hell. The soldiers play dice in the bottom right hand corner with a callous greed. Their dice and their drum of war are the most identifiable objects in the picture. On the left is a powerful, gruesome figure that threatens like a Tyrannosaurus Rex. It seems to have the purple cape of an Imperial Roman Official. Perhaps this is the power of the state

– it stands astride what seems to be a classical pedimented facade. The whole picture is red and yellow creating a sense of immense fire and heat around the grey, ashen figure of Christ. Could this be the heat of war, the Spanish Civil War perhaps (the date is right), the searing heat of a bullet or a village set alight and the grey Christ as it were cremated by it?

There is a shaft of hope in the picture in the form of a ladder, enormously long like Jacob's ladder. You see a ladder in many a traditional crucifixion scene, as a means one assumes for the soldiers to climb up to the transverse beam of the cross, but this one has numerous rungs and leads from the despair of broken bodies at the base to a figure who looks as if he or she is about to climb out of this hell into heaven.

So I think it is a commentary on our suffering, how each generation suffers the agony that Christ suffered. Like any good work of art it doesn't so much answer questions as ask them.

My third picture was painted by Gilbert Spencer in 1915. It shows five white-shirted young men elevating the cross by standing in a line behind and pushing up against the cross beam. The Christ figure is traditional and could be taken from a medieval painting or perhaps might be a crucifix being erected at a roadside such as you see in France or Spain. Certainly the figure on the cross is not contemporary with the men lifting it. It strikes me as a commentary on human violence and the violence that is within us. What I see in this picture is the idea that modern people participate in the crucifixion and that Christ is, as it were, crucified over and over again by each generation. Reading the Gospel story it is very easy, psychologically, to transfer the blame for what is done to Jesus onto the religious fanatics of the time, or Pilate's weakness, as if to say it's nothing to do with us, it's the political system. The same kind of passing the buck that we have today. But this picture says, no, it's you. Your own clean-cut young men are doing this still. I guess because of the date – in the First World War – there is more than a hint of young civilians becoming soldiers and going off to the killing field of Flanders. It's a pity the picture doesn't show women and men, young and old, but the point is made. 'Were you there when they crucified my Lord? Were you there when they nailed him to the tree?' If so what did you do about it? Did you object, or did you join in?

The power of the story in the New Testament is that once he had been arrested Jesus was left utterly alone. The disciples fled and even his closest disciple, Peter, denied having known him. This utter dereliction is symbolised most forcefully at the end of the Eucharist on the Thursday night before Good Friday when the congregation traditionally leaves in silence – no chatting, no shaking hands with the priest, no comment on the quality of the sermon – everyone is complicit with what is being done to Christ.

Forgiveness

So the discussion turns back to the initial question about salvation – being saved from what? – and the answers given by a group of students, ranging from 'being saved from our sins' to 'being saved from ourselves'. Those simple answers, like the story of Adam and Eve, recognise that there is a pervasive selfishness in human beings that plays havoc with our relationships, personally, nationally, and internationally. At its most extreme this selfishness can lead to violence and murder, and at the political level to such aberrations as apartheid and ethnic cleansing.

From the Christian point of view how is this to be dealt with? The first point that Jesus makes is that everyone should see that they are implicated in human wrongdoing. He says this in the Sermon on the Mount in Matthew Chapter Five that evil is not just what *other people* do. He argues that anger is the root of murder, sexual lust the root of adultery, and that we should recognise the potential damage that these common feelings can cause. The point he is making is that it's not such a huge step from a family row to a bread knife thrust into a chest, from envy to robbery, or from nationalism to ethnic cleansing. The line between controlled and uncontrolled behaviour can be wafer thin and the selfishness in *you* is just as bad as the selfishness in the sinners who hit the headlines.

How can this selfishness be dealt with? By repentance of the sort Jesus calls for at the beginning of his ministry. John the Baptist had been preparing the ground calling people to be baptised as a sign of repentance. When Jesus came on the scene he said, 'The time is fulfilled, and the kingdom of God has come near; repent, and believe in the good news.' He didn't offer a complicated theological formula, he just wanted a simple straightforward response.

So how does the repentance that Jesus teaches work?

1. Having the self-understanding to know that you've done wrong is half the battle. One version of the Bible translates Jesus' words, 'Blessed are the poor in Spirit' as 'How blest are those who know their need of God', and that sums it up very neatly.
2. Repentance requires a person to be sorry for what they have done wrong, for conscience to speak, and for there to be a sense of remorse.
3. The next step is to make amends. Can the wrong be righted? What reme-

dial steps can be taken? It is not enough simply to feel remorse; you need actively to seek reconciliation, to make repayment, or to heal wounds. This is what Desmond Tutu tried to achieve in South Africa with the Truth and Reconciliation Movement. The hearings sought to examine some of the key events and personalities involved in apartheid, to try to establish the truth behind those stories and to reconcile people through honesty and apology.

4. There is a fourth aspect to the repentance process, which is different but related. It looks at the problem from the other side, from the point of view of the person *sinned against*. One of Jesus' most controversial demands was to turn the other cheek. 'If someone strikes you on one cheek turn the other also and if someone steals your coat give them your cloak as well'. When the disciples ask him how many times they should forgive their enemies, they suggest seven times, thinking that this is massively good-hearted, but Jesus replies no, seventy times seven! This attitude runs through the whole of his teaching and lifestyle. He teaches that revenge, rancour, and bitterness, although perfectly understandable, are in the end counter-productive.

Over the centuries many saintly Christians have managed to put this demanding teaching into practice. Leonard Wilson, who was Anglican Bishop of Birmingham, is one who comes to mind. During the Second World War he had been imprisoned and tortured in Singapore. Later, as a bishop he confirmed one of his torturers as a member of the Church. It's hard to imagine what it would be like to lay your hands on the head of someone who had tortured you and driven you mad with fear and say the words, 'Defend, O Lord, this thy servant with thy heavenly grace, that he may continue thine for ever'? It's a remarkable turn around and reminds us of Jesus' own attitude to his executioners, 'Father forgive them for they know not what they do.' The story also serves as a parable for how demanding reconciliation can be. There are no cheap and easy solutions to the problems created by selfishness and cruelty, but if you go out of your way to apologise and put things right, most people will immediately be ready to forgive and to repair any damage that has been done.

This is a concrete example of what I understand by salvation and it is my answer to the question, how are we saved. Repentance and reconciliation are the essence of salvation and when they are achieved people are in a real sense saved from their sins and from the innate selfishness that dominates our personalities. The result is very positive and creative and allows people to start again and rebuild the damaged parts of their lives.

The final question is whether any of this happens on the big scale between God and human beings; whether it makes sense to speak of an invisible God forgiving sins or being reconciled to people. I have said that I don't accept that sin is overthrown in a cosmic battle between good and evil, or indeed that the death and resurrection of Jesus works in that kind of way. There is too much evidence to the contrary: people (and places) scarred physically and mentally, often beyond repair, by man's inhumanity to man. But I do believe that the Christian story points to love's power to transform both at the individual level, as in the case of Bishop Wilson, and at the transcendent level as represented by Christ. At the transcendent level I believe God is what Charles Wesley called 'Great Universal Love'. God is the potential of love in creation, and reveals this bias to love through Jesus – as Paul says his second letter to the Corinthians, 'God was in Christ reconciling the world to himself'. What is saving and forgiving about God is the simple fact that his creation is charged with the endless potential for reconciliation, forgiveness, putting the past right and starting afresh.

In this sense salvation is something people can tune into or not, as the case may be, and it rather makes redundant the old question of who gets saved and whether salvation is for everyone or the chosen few. Personally I have a strong dislike of the kind of Christianity that emphasises divine privileges for Christians that no one else can enjoy. Basically, it just doesn't appeal and it has never been one of the motivating forces that makes me a Christian. I am not a Christian because I want pie in the sky when I die, but because instinctively I believe in God and I have an enormous admiration for the character of the Jesus who steps out of the pages of the New Testament. I can see that the lifestyle he promotes is fulfilling and that it expresses what is ultimately important. That is enough for me. I also recognise that many of the ideals taught by Christianity are shared by people who are not religious at all, or adhere to other religions and I could not put my hand on my heart and say that I believe that they cannot find salvation too.

Is Christianity exclusive or inclusive?

Let's look at the question of whether Christianity is the only way to God. Certainly, it has a record of being rather exclusive. The Book of Revelation suggests that only the 144,000 whose names are written in the Book of Life can be saved. Jesus said, 'I am the way, the truth and the life, no one comes to the Father but by me' and also very decisively that 'those who are not with me are against me'.

On the other hand he could be radically inclusive for his time. He welcomed children with the famous words, suffer the little children and let them come to me; he welcomed women, and notoriously allowed a woman to anoint his feet in public and wipe them with her hair. He had contact with lepers, who were regarded as untouchable, and healed one by the laying on of hands. He told the religious pietists that he was more interested in sinners, tax gatherers, and prostitutes than he was in them. Christianity had begun as a Jewish sect, but very soon after the resurrection it was recognised that non-Jews must be included as members. So on balance I consider the gospel precedent inclusive rather than exclusive. Nevertheless, Jesus' statement that no one comes to the Father but by him weighs very heavily with a lot of Christians. Many's the time I have preached in favour of inclusivity only to have that text bounced back at me at the door by an agitated member of the congregation. The solution is to read the text in an inclusive way – if anyone comes to God, they come via Christ, even if not consciously. How can *that* be?

When you mention *Christ* most people automatically think of *Jesus*, but the New Testament claims that Christ is *more than* the historical person of Jesus of Nazareth. For example John's Gospel holds that Christ is the eternal Word of God, which existed from the beginning of time. This is a much more philosophical interpretation of Christ: he is not simply the bloke who caused a stir in Galilee, but the innate goodness of creation. John actually says that *through him all things were made.* In other words Christly goodness pervades everything, and whenever a person acts lovingly they are in touch with God and God's eternal Word *whether they know it or not.* You might say that all aspirations to goodness lead to God and therefore, in Christian language, to Christ the eternal Word of God. This is definitely not an argument to claim that Muslims, Jews and Hindus are really Christians after all, but don't know it. That would be ridiculous and arrogant. It is more a statement that God's transcendence necessarily goes beyond the petty divisions of human institutions: no church can contain God, and no one can claim exclusive knowledge or privilege of God.

So why is religion so divisive?

On the evidence of Jesus' teaching it would be reasonable to think that Christianity is about turning the other cheek, loving your enemy, being reconciled with neighbours, and making peace, but in practice it has had a long and complex history of violence and division. Take for instance the Crusades against Islam, the Spanish Inquisition, the burning of Catholics and Protestants as heretics in the 16th century, the witch trials of Salem in America (made famous by Arthur Miller's play *The Crucible*), and Catholic and Protestant terrorism in Ireland. You might also say, because Christianity was the formative religion of Europe, that it was complicit in the persecution of Jews by Hitler and as the predominant religion of America it is a major force in the current war between the West and Islam.

Why does Christianity and religion in general encourage division and war?

First there are theological reasons. The inclusiveness I argued for just now is inevitably loose-ended but there is a strong vein running through religion that is hostile to loose ends; people want answers, they want to know where they stand on matters of belief and morals. I am not unsympathetic to this because obviously there have to be basic defining principles that mark out Christianity. It has to have shape and structure. At the most obvious level it would seem to me impossible to be a Christian without believing that God is revealed in Jesus Christ. Sometimes parents bringing their child for baptism want to have a non-Christian friend as a godparent and I always feel obliged to refuse because the service requires godparents to affirm their belief in Jesus Christ. However, the desire for clear-cut answers can all too quickly turn to dogmatism and dogmatism, if one is not careful, to fanaticism. This is the Achilles heel of religion; a weakness that spoils so much of the good that religion achieves. The psychology of it seems to be related to the fear of the death of religion on the part of believers. There is no doubt that in the liberal West Christianity is under threat from secularisation, which is radically critical of the intellectual claims of Christianity, starting with belief in God. One natural reaction against this is to adopt a siege mentality and retreat into more and more extreme positions, maintaining beliefs in the face of all opposition as a kind of flag of identity. A typical example would be the support of six day creation versus evolution in which a literal belief in the events of creation as told in the Bible is pitted against the account given by physics and biology. This is not to imply that liberal Christianity is untouched by the effect of secularisation, far from it, but that there can be other strategies of response than out and out opposition.

Another reason for confrontational attitudes in religion is that religions are about God and God is understood to be all knowing and all powerful and therefore always right. To know God's will, and to be able to cite God's will in support of your cause, seems to give absolute authority – at least you might think so. But how do you know God's will? From sacred texts, from sacred persons such as the Pope, from prayer, from doctrines, from the majority vote of church committees? God's will is always discerned through interpretation and the interpretation varies! Theological clashes arise, usually in good faith, from different interpretations of the same original material. If I were to take a vote in my congregation on whether the bread and wine of the Eucharist is actually or symbolically the body and blood of Christ probably one half would say yes and the other half would say no. Is it theologically acceptable for women to be priests? Does the sanctity of human life created by God make it immoral to experiment with human embryos? These are all theological issues on which the Church is divided and which arouse deep emotions.

Then there are political reasons – although it can be very difficult to disentangle the political from the theological! To what extent does one drive the other? This is clearest in the issue of territory: can religion justify the possession of land or does the political desire for land motivate the religious support? Look at the problem of Israel and the Middle East. The Jews believe the land of Israel was promised to them by God in the Old Testament and is therefore theirs by divine right. Conservative American Christians support this view on Biblical grounds. Whereas the Palestinian Muslims say, this is ours by long tenure; we are the sitting tenants. Jerusalem is an important holy site for us too. People fight for the land they believe God has given them.

But it's not only Israel; there's something of the *Holy Land* mentality in the British and American psyches too. The Americans refer to their land as 'God's own country' and in a much quoted speech from Richard III Shakespeare describes England as 'this scepter'd isle',

> 'This blessed plot, this earth, this realm, this England,
> This nurse, this teeming womb of royal kings,
> Renowned for their deeds as far from home,
> For Christian service and true chivalry,
> As is the sepulchre in stubborn Jewry
> Of the world's ransom, blessed Mary's Son ...'

This anti-Semitic speech (stubborn Jewry) suggests that England is land given by God to the English who rule over it by divine right, and although the language is distinctly Elizabethan, the sentiments are familiar today.

The emotive force of this sense of possession of the land suggests that religion is wrapped up with our sense of identity and the preservation of our identity. In the modern world these identities are as strong as ever: we speak of Muslim, Christian, Jewish and Hindu nations, and ethnic groups in exile often work particularly hard to maintain their cultural identity. When I worked in North London I taught 'A level' RE to some of the children of the Greek Cypriot community. My students were thoroughly modern young women, but occasionally on Sundays they were taken by their parents, or more likely their grandparents, to the Greek Orthodox church where they heard the gospel read in an old Greek that they didn't understand. But the important thing was that this ritual preserved their cultural identity in a foreign land. They were being asked to remember that above all they were Greek Cypriots. This as it happens was not divisive, but we know that in other British cities – Belfast, Leicester, Bradford – the isolationist policies of religious cultural groups has led to violence and civil unrest.

Basically we are all driven by the instinct for self-preservation and Christianity doesn't escape that drive however much it teaches self-sacrifice. Just as a parent fights to protect a child, so people will fight for the protection of an idea or a social order; and since religion always develops in a cultural setting it is bound to reflect the values and needs of that culture.

Another issue that divides people on religious grounds is sexuality. Why does homosexuality, marriage, women's dress, abortion, contraception, celibacy, women priests, and embryo research provoke such strong divisions of opinion amongst religious people? For some their whole psychological, political, and social self-understanding is summed up by the position they take on these issues, whether it is the Muslim woman wearing her veil or the pro-life campaigner demonstrating outside an abortion clinic.

I think the reason why sexuality can be so divisive is that religion likes order and social cohesion and fears deviation. Hence the prominence of law codes like the Ten Commandments and the desire for clear cut rules, the function of which at their best are liberating – the emphasis in Christianity on marriage, or in Islam on modest dress for women, is intended to support a social order in which relationships can flourish and children can be secure – but at their worst are repressive and life-denying.

Similarly, embryo research and any interference with the so-called 'natural' process of reproduction creates fears about loss of human dignity, and also of what you might call the Frankenstein effect – the fear of our own power, that scientific advance might turn round to destroy us. We are frightened that new technologies will actually allow us to *modify* ourselves and therefore change our identities with unpredictable consequences, possibly endangering our hold on meaning and fulfilment. The book of Genesis says that humankind is made in the *image of God* and that idea provides the theological rationale for conservatism. Don't tamper with God's image!

So religion, culture and politics are mixed up together in the battle for self-identity as we try to answer Alice in Wonderland's universal question 'Who in the world am I?'. It is hardly surprising if in the process we become protective because identity is such a fragile and hard fought for thing, especially in a plural world. This need for identity and answers to the mystery of life is surely the chief psychological factor that pushes people towards fundamentalism; this need for black and white, clear-cut answers; this abhorrence of deviation from the norm; this rejection of risk for the sake of knowing-where-you-stand.

The theologian Karen Armstrong says that the fundamentalism evident in every major faith shows that many people all over the world want their leaders to speak out with clear-cut teaching. But, she also says that fundamentalism distorts the faith it is trying to preserve and therefore represents a defeat for religion. But how come defeat, when worldwide the religious groups that are expanding most are the fundamentalist ones, or at least those with very conservative tendencies? The point is, extremism strangles the life out of the faith it is trying to preserve by being intellectually, and often morally, restrictive. It does this not out of malice, of course, but with the intention of eliminating doubt and making faith easier. Would it were so simple. The Christianity I believe in forces me to live in a tension between a settled and a radically different community. On the one hand it supports the existence of rules and values, but on the other it always challenges those rules and values. Jesus was far from the suburban man with a settled job and a stable way of life. 'Foxes have holes, and birds of the air have nests,' he said of himself, 'but the Son of Man has nowhere to lay his head.' He promoted the law and values of God, but at the same time he questioned the customs and values of his day, such as Sabbath day observance, the use of the Temple and the rituals that surrounded it, and the social status of women. He was a prophetic figure and the characteristic of a prophet is to be a part of a society, yet to stand outside it in critical judgement. So paradoxically, Jesus' religion, which I have argued is inclusive and open, was itself provocative and divisive. Jesus spoke of bringing the *sword of division*, which was a way of saying that he recognised the provocative nature of what he was proposing. When he told a would-be follower who wanted first to bury his father to let the dead bury their dead, he was demanding the kind of commitment that divides families. And of course his behaviour generally, whether it was healing on the Sabbath, dining with tax collectors, accusing the religious Jews of hypocrisy, or turning over the tables of the moneychangers in the Temple, was the very thing that got him crucified.

Yet we think of Christ as a conciliator and a symbol of unity. In G W Briggs' hymn, 'Christ is the World's true light' there is a verse that says, 'In Christ all races meet, their ancient feuds forgetting'. This is a sentiment that reflects the Christian imperialism of the 19th century more than any actual historical experience, but it nevertheless expresses the Christian hope that ultimately God will reconcile the whole creation to himself. Meanwhile, for Christ to have an impact, Christians need to follow his example. If he lowered his guard and self-defence in order to proclaim the truth, shouldn't we do the same, and isn't this how we might live together?

7.
Why does God allow suffering?

Suffering is one of the biggest paradoxes of our culture. Medical advance has seduced us into thinking it can be eliminated, and yet it surrounds us in pervasive and awful ways. We sanitise it in hospital wards, and mask it with brilliant analgesic cocktails and anti-depressant drugs. Genetic research promises us ways of replacing and restoring diseased tissue and organs in a medical revolution that will increase the average life span to a hundred years and more, at least for those able to afford the treatment. At the same time satellite communication beams instantaneous images of suffering and violence into our living rooms on a scale that we haven't seen before. Communication is so immediate that wars are watched in progress and on 11 September 2001 the terrorist attack on the World Trade Center in New York was screened live. In an ironic way, however, this bombardment with images of violence feeds the end-of-suffering myth because the two-dimensional TV presentation is essentially reductionist – the pain, the smell, the extremes of temperature are absent. TV looks in from the outside without feeling what it is like to be the victim at the centre. While other people fight for their lives, the viewer sits comfortably and munches an apple.

But for all this kidology about the end-of-suffering, for all the conventional and alternative therapies and advertising that invites you to pamper yourself with shampoos, cosmetics and scented candles, all the cocooning in centrally heated houses and virtual reality, for everything that pretends suffering can be eliminated, violence, pain and mental illness are there, irrevocably taunting us with our mortality and frailty, and we don't like it.

Of course I shouldn't be morally patronising about this. An important part of the Christian tradition looks forward to a future paradise in which pain and suffering are eliminated and there are some beautiful passages in the Bible that describe it. For example the reading from Isaiah chapter 11 used in many

Christmas Carol services, which speaks of the coming of a righteous judge who will bring in an era of peace when the lion will lie down with the lamb and children will be able to play without fear of snakes. 'They shall not hurt or destroy in all my holy mountain'. Or there's the passage in the Book of Revelation (21:4) where John the Divine dreams of God's kingdom and says that God will wipe away every tear. 'Death will be no more; mourning and crying and pain will be no more, for the first things have passed away.'

But to continue my argument, if the high tech, hedonistic life style of the First World has tempted us to think of suffering as a feature of man's primitive condition that now ought to be eliminated, religion feels the same cultural blast. Whereas once suffering had to be accepted and even regarded as an ennobling and improving experience, now it seems a scandal that God should allow suffering at all.

This has become the major objection to belief in God: how can an all-powerful and all-loving God allow suffering? Either he is not all-powerful or he is not all-loving. The atheist takes up the theme with relish, suggesting that since the universe shows pitiless indifference to suffering, it is not the sort of universe that one would expect if there were a God. Game, set and match! It's a strong argument, and made even stronger because so many Christians and theists sympathise with it. Even the most secure faith can be shaken when confronted with bitter experience such as the loss of a child, the onset of cancer, or a suicide bomb and it is understandable that people sometimes blame God. It's a natural thing to do. If God created us, why shouldn't he be responsible for the things that happen to us? Of the many examples I can think of, one sticks in my mind: a thoughtful and talented academic couple who were devoted church members until discovering that their youngest child was mentally handicapped. It was such a torment to them that they left the Church in protest. Their departure was an accusation against God, a shout of pain that I found both moving and understandable. I had to respect where they were in their wilderness of disaffection with God.

But that is the negative side. On the positive side, in my experience as a priest, I would say that I've seen more suffering people turn *to* God than away *from* God. This is not surprising since statistics show that distress is one of the most common triggers of religious experience. For example, the onset of suffering can provoke an instinctive recourse to prayer – the instinctive 'O my God' or 'God help me'. Or suffering can be the wake-up-call that makes a person take their relationships more seriously and more lovingly. Illness or the loss of a loved one often shocks us into asking those ultimate questions about what values matter most. It creates a spiritual alertness and sensitivity that can easily elude us when life is bowling along without a care in the world.

Two friends of my eighteen-year-old daughter were killed in a car crash just before Christmas. Their eighteen-year-old lives were all fun, travel, university, clubs, careers, and parties. Then bang. Suddenly the group of friends are faced with death and their own mortality. They can't believe it. How can young lives that were just beginning suddenly be over? Through the grief and the shock the friends left behind are forced to ask, perhaps for the first time, what really matters to them, what's really important.

Although most of that eighteen-year-old peer group would probably describe themselves as agnostic, the most natural way of marking the death of their friends was to hold a service in church. They sang hymns, said prayers and young person after young person stood up to give a testimony to the life of their friend. It was a way of honouring those lives, but also a way of expressing the almost inexpressible seriousness with which they experienced this bereavement and the sense that some of them had of a being that transcended their youthful values and appalling loss. Thus, an instinctive turning to God provided not just consolation and a focus for their emotion, but a purpose to give them hope beyond the tragedy. People look to religion to get them through suffering so that they are not destroyed by it.

The case is strengthened too by the clear evidence of the response to 11 September 2001. Rather than turning away from God or blaming God, there was a massive influx of people coming to pray in churches. When, three days later, there was a nationally observed three-minute silence, my central Oxford church filled up with about three hundred people, some sitting and kneeling, but many just standing at the back unsure what they were doing. I had received many phone calls prior to the occasion saying that people wanted more than the silence; they wanted prayer and reflection and the reading of Scripture, which was what we provided. At a time of acute public suffering and fear, people turned to God and gravitated towards churches in the hope of finding that transcendence.

Suffering is the necessary cost of life

As I write this chapter I have been visiting a 97-year-old dying man. He was a benevolent and gracious doctor, dignified and old-fashioned, immensely kind to his patients. I had only ever know him in a suit with his shock of white hair meticulously brushed, but now he lay naked and skeletal on the bed struggling for breath, having pushed away the bedclothes because he felt so hot. It was a final torment and when his poor old body gave up the struggle and he relaxed in death and I saw the power of that poetry: crying and pain will be no more, for the first things have passed away. He never complained and often said to me in his last years that he had 'fought the good fight'.

It strikes me as absurd to think of pain and suffering as wholly bad, or indeed to imagine a God who sees (or *ought* to see) pain as wholly bad. Nietzsche considered the matter over a long period and eventually argued that fulfilment is not reached by avoiding pain but by recognising its role as a natural, inevitable step on the way to reaching anything good. In fact suffering is an inevitable feature of the wonderful life that God has created.

Increasing knowledge of the universe makes us realise what a miracle it is that life exists at all: most places are too hot, or too cold, or too poisonous, or too dry, or without the right gravitational pull to sustain it. The fact that there is life on Earth depends on a remarkable balance of immense natural forces such as the balance of oxygen to carbon dioxide, the planets' distance from the sun, and the protective effect of the ozone layer against the radiation of the sun. Slight variations to these conditions would make life impossible. And we fragile humans beings frequently take life for granted oblivious to the enormity of where we come from. The movement of the earth's crust, with consequent earthquakes and volcanoes, reminds us of the immense forces that underpin life itself. These natural and violent events are typical of the physical conditions that make life possible in the first place. The universe came into being through the violence of the 'Big Bang' and, according to one theory, life cells first reached earth as the result of a violent collision with a meteor – the same kind of collision that destroyed the dinosaurs. Creation itself is a potentially violent business and a telling parable for it is the pain of childbirth. No life without pain! The nature and process of physical existence is one of change and decay and re-cycling and transformation of matter through birth, reproduction and death – and this process involves pain and suffering. It is the unavoidable way of life: our freedom to move can result in collision, the cells that make our beautiful bodies can abnormally multiply as cancerous growths, and the energy that can enhance life – electricity, nuclear, the sea, the sun – can also destroy it. All the beauty we see, the love we experience, and the hope we have, comes at this necessary cost.

Although I speak of suffering as a necessary *cost* of life in God's creation, it would be misguided to think of it in wholly negative terms. For example, pain has obvious practical uses that support life. It is an early warning system signalling when the body is sick or injured and in need of attention: the thorn must be extracted or it festers, the wound must be cleaned and stitched. Without such pain the body is in great danger as in the case of Leprosy – a disease that destroys the superficial nerve endings. The consequent lack of feeling in the hands and feet results in damage and disfigurement particularly by unnoticed burns and knocks. The body needs sensation, of which pain is a part, to survive. I have often thought that torture is a peculiar evil precisely because it's a calculated abuse of this natural, beneficial mechanism.

My conclusion is that God could not have created things any different! God creates within a framework of possible being. To argue that an all-powerful God could have invented and created any sort of world he liked, and why didn't he do it differently, seems perverse. In any case the picture of God as the divine mathematician – the inventor of physics and biochemistry – begs some questions about the nature of his creativity. I would prefer to understand God's creative energy in terms of relationship building rather than design and technology. God creates within the context of being and when he revealed his love in Jesus Christ, he did so in a life the living of which has suffering as a necessary condition and consequence. Moreover, as we have repeatedly observed, the divine nature is expressed precisely in the way in which Jesus copes with suffering and conflict.

Suffering as revelation and relationship building

I suggest that in contemporary experience God's nature is recognised through relationships, especially as they move through suffering and conflict to reconciliation and fulfilment. The best example of this is summed up in Jesus' words: no one has greater love than this, to lay down one's life for one's friends. Immediately I think of the love of a parent who would rather die than see their child harmed, or the courage of a soldier in battle or a fire-fighter in an emergency, such as the terrorist attack on New York's twin towers, who dies in the process of saving others. We sometimes call this the 'ultimate sacrifice' and we see it as a model for the love of God, which is specifically revealed in the death of Jesus, where the innocent man suffers for the sins of the guilty. Thus, not only is suffering a necessary biological cost of life, but the very suffering that we initially regarded as immensely suspect in the divine scale of things actually mediates our ideas of what it is to be God.

Often the revelation comes through the surprise factor in a story. In his wonderful book *Humanity*, Jonathan Glover, writing from an atheist point of view, cites two stories that show how tribal barriers can be broken down. From my Christian point of view I would use them as pointers to God. The first is a childhood memory of Desmond Tutu in apartheid-ridden South Africa. Uneducated black women in that society counted for very little and so Tutu was quite taken aback when one day a white priest doffed his cap to Mrs Tutu in greeting. The priest was Fr Trevor Huddleston. Tutu says that the moment left a deep impression that made him realise he was precious in the sight of God and 'helped him not become anti-white'.

The second story, from sectarian Northern Ireland, was told by Seamus Heaney of a group of workmen held up by masked men. The Catholics were told to step out, but all were protestant except one. They assumed the masked men were Protestants. One of the Protestant men squeezed the hand of the Catholic in a gesture that said, we won't betray you. But the man stepped out, was pushed to one side, and the others were shot. The terrorists were from the IRA. The story can only have become known through the testimony of the Catholic the Protestant tried to save, and this is what gives it its prophetic force.

So godliness is seen in relationship and if you want a specific theology for this it is the theology of the Holy Trinity, that puzzling but basically straightforward idea that God is revealed as Father, Son, and Holy Spirit. The doctrine of the Trinity seems to be saying that God is identifiable by relationship, that there is an ongoing set of relationships at the heart of God. The father/son bit is fairly obvious: the creator God is like a father and the incarnate God, Jesus, is his son. In prayer Jesus speaks of God as Father, as in the Lord's Prayer – 'our father who art in heaven'. And in the crucifixion story the father/son tension of relationship is unmistakable when Jesus prays, 'Father, if it be your will take this cup from me, nevertheless not my will but yours be done'. However, God is not restricted to this father/son model. God is also Holy Spirit, or, as you might say, God in each of us. This third dimension is very important because it means that God's relational activity is not merely internal to the Godhead but opened out to humanity in a plural and inclusive way, so that the possibilities of encountering God are endless. Of course, in the process of trying to make the idea of the Trinity work, you don't want to take the analogous language of relationship too literally or God becomes a puzzle like a 'Rubik's Cube' which once you have mixed it up is excessively hard to reconfigure.

I find it helpful to compare my theological understanding of suffering and relationship with my understanding of how suffering, extremity, and relationship influences art. What, for example, makes for compelling television or good theatre? The answer is the dramatic tension of how people resolve or fail to resolve the experience of broken relationship, failure, and disappointment.

Watching other people grapple with these problems is therapeutic because it helps us refine the art of relationship in our own lives. The most gripping story lines in the soaps are when you are left wondering how a couple will make their relationship work against the odds. *Friends, Sex in the City,* and *Frasier* are all long running sitcoms whose success depends on the struggle of their characters in the stormy sea of troubled relationship. In higher art, in Shakespeare's tragedies for example, the themes are exactly the same: how a jealous man loses his young wife over the irrational suspicion of a handkerchief found in the possession of another man (Othello), how political ambition leads to murder and revenge (Macbeth), how a moneylender's failure to show mercy results in his losing his land and his daughter (The Merchant of Venice).

Suffering is the inspiration and catalyst of art. It is not these bare boned plots, but how they are dealt with, how we resolve the suffering and the failure and the broken relationship, that is at the nub of human fulfilment, of religion and the understanding of God. Hence Nietzsche's claim that pain is an inevitable step on the way to reaching anything good.

The shock of God-forsakenness

Nevertheless, having said all this, even the Son of God experienced the atheistic shock wave that suffering can cause when he cried out from the cross, 'my God why hast thou forsaken me?' It is a key moment in the Christian story because of its total honesty. We do not see a Son of God for whom suffering is a matter of effortless ease, a superman who takes suffering in his stride and sort of zaps it. If he has any victory over suffering it is by accepting it, struggling with it, and being broken by it. In words taken from Isaiah, and applied to Jesus, he is seen as despised and rejected, a man of sorrows and acquainted with grief. Christ's experience is in solidarity with ours and it would be bland to pretend, as people sometimes do, that for those who believe in God suffering ought to be lightly borne or that everything will be alright in the end. Much suffering is unresolved, unredeemed, relentless and bitterly incomprehensible: incurable pain, ethnic cleansing, terrorist atrocity, calculated torture, the sense of vulnerable loneliness when you realise that your pain must be borne by you alone. All this, as we've seen, makes the popular and penetrating case against God.

What Christianity does say, however, is that the god-forsaken cry of the crucifixion embraces that suffering. As the writer to the Hebrews (2:18) argues, 'because Christ was tested by what he suffered, he is able to help those who are being tested'. Not that the Passion of Christ necessarily makes pain easier to bear or to understand, but that God shows solidarity with our experience at its most dire and most unbearable. Yet there are many people who cannot accept even that. And this is where faith comes in and why faith is so difficult. It is not always easy to believe that God is present in the depth of despair. In Barbara Kingsolver's wonderful novel *The Poisonwood Bible* the missionary's daughter, fleeing from a plague of ants in the Congolese jungle, says at a pivotal moment 'when I walk through the valley of the shadow the Lord is supposed to be with me, and he is not'.

I only really discovered this for myself when I had to go into hospital for a neurological operation that could have left me in a wheelchair – but thankfully didn't. Before that I had preached about suffering with the glib naivety of someone who had never really suffered anything traumatic. For years I have visited people in hospital as part of my job and seen them enduring the most awful illnesses and personal trials, but I remained immune to the harsher realities, not unfeeling, I hope, but professionally detached – even from death. At the end of the day the visitor is always able to walk away from the curtained beds and cut flowers, along the lime green corridors into the street, grateful for the traffic and the movement of life.

Being a patient changes all this. Suddenly imprisoned in a ward, privacy and freedom are taken away and replaced by apprehension and uncertainty – the 'welcome' leaflet on the locker beside my bed included a paragraph that assured me that among the many services offered was the undertaking to help patients 'die with dignity'. The plight of the other patients is now your own plight, not a remote and escapable condition – you're all in the same boat. You feel so tense that your blood pressure shoots up out of the normal range, yet you're too shy to admit that your thoughts are at all apocalyptic as you put on a brave face.

The night I was admitted the surgeons came round and explained in graphic detail to each of us what surgical procedures would be required. The man opposite me had a brain tumour that would require to be accessed both through the skull and through the nasal cavity. The description was so horrendous it made me weep and he kept saying, 'I don't want to know, just do it'. But the patient must give 'informed' consent and be aware that in this case there was a fifteen per cent chance of dying under anaesthetic.

The challenge that this suffering placed at God's door hit me with the force of a head on collision. It couldn't be argued away and it was spirituality less than congenial. It was a simple fact and quite a shock to me as a priest. It is often said that priests make bad patients in hospital!

I had been given Martin Amis' autobiography *Experience* for Christmas and this was the book I read in hospital. It was my choice, but not to be recommended in the circumstances! It's about the critical, turning points of experience, which he calls the *main events*. The *main events* are those events that accompany one's departure from this world and the significant moments that prefigure it, such as Philip Larkin's evocative plea in a letter to Kingsley Amis, 'Remember me as I pack my pyjamas and shaving things for the great ordeal'.

This was my first main event and each of us in my sub-section of the ward were in our different ways learning about what Amis called the 'weakness of our life tenure' – to which he added, and 'the lack of cosmic support for it.' That of course is the atheist speaking – the lack of cosmic support for our weakness. Christianity has to beware of being glib in response. It has offered some unconvincing compensations in this department. There's a good time coming: pie in the sky when you die. Part of everyone's mortality – their main events – is facing up to personal dispensability. However much others try to help, there is an essential loneliness to suffering, it's inside *you*, you have got to cope, life will go on with relentless, even rapacious, vigour whatever happens to you.

But just to complete the circle of this particular section of the discussion, something struck me very strongly in the TV coverage of the events of September 11, 2001. It was the exclamation of a fireman coincidentally filmed looking up at the World Trade Centre as the first plane hit: 'Holy Shit', he said. It's language that shocks uttered by a shocked individual. It catches the paradox of what I have been saying; the sacred and secular are combined in an instinctive shout, 'holy shit' – God and yet not God! In an ironical way the apparent blasphemies uttered in extreme situations call on God's presence – 'Christ', 'Oh, my God'. The response to an absent God is often an instinctive appeal to God.

Does God suffer?

At some level the question seems absurd. If you think of God as immortal, invisible, and omnipotent, then how can God suffer? Surely only creatures of flesh and blood suffer, and a transcendent God must be beyond suffering. But the seemingly common sense question doesn't always illuminate the problem. I'd draw a comparison with the way I try to understand what physicists are saying about the universe. I ask what seem like common sense questions – such as, if the universe is expanding what is it expanding into? Intuitively I assume the universe is *in* some larger space, and find it difficult to conceive that the universe can be *all that there is*. But physicists tell me I can't simply apply my everyday ideas of three dimensional space and time moving from past to future to the unthinkably large universe where time and light bend and 'dark matter' is hidden. What God and the outer universe have in common is that once we have exhausted the possibilities of everyday language they can only be spoken about theoretically or experimentally. Instead of being up there, or out there, or somewhere, God is in all or through all. The transcendent God might be *beyond* our experience but is *in* all that is. Only in the ancient three tier-model of the universe is it possible to have God in a place called heaven at a notionally measurable distance from us.

The question I want to ask – and it can only be a question or a tentative proposal – is that when we speak of the transcendent God, are we claiming that there is a cosmic meaning or purpose, a cosmic empathy or compassion? Is that what is meant by the famous line in the New Testament, 'God so loved the world …'? Is there a divine compassion or is creation, as atheists would argue, coldly indifferent to suffering?

I think of God by analogy with my experience as a parent. Let's say your teen-age child falls in love and is jilted. The pain of a broken relationship can be es-pecially devastating for a teenager, magnified as it is by super active hormones. There's little as a parent you can do or say, but you feel the anguish as if it were your own. That is empathetic suffering, compassion, *suffering with* someone else. And I want to propose a God who feels empathetic suffering for creation even if there's little God can do or say.

I have attempted to make an abstract case, but of course Christianity has a concrete answer: the suffering of Christ in the final days of his life is the suffer-ing of God. The life of Jesus is a model of divine love that feels our pain and suffers with us.

God is in the wound not in the bandage

The genius of Christianity is that God's being *in all* is symbolised by the incar-nation. God is poured into the bodily experience. The extravagant claim is that all the 'fullness of God' is poured into one person, an individual, for the sake of argument let's say a five foot six, eleven stone man. Then this man is nailed to a cross so he can't move his arms or legs. That concentration of Godness is tortured and lives through everyone's worst nightmare: disablement, humilia-tion, extreme and sustained pain. As in all these discussions there is no com-plete explanation, but the Christian belief is that God's suffering in this way is redemptive and it makes a difference. The difference is made because God is, as it were, in the wound not in the bandage. That's a phrase I find particularly helpful in trying to understand the mystery of suffering. God's identification with human suffering is not in patching up but being in the cancer and in the wounds inflicted by the torturer, bearing them with you.

St Paul says in Romans Chapter Five that 'suffering produces endurance, and endurance produces character, and character produces hope, and hope does not disappoint us, because God's love has been poured into our hearts through the Holy Spirit that has been given to us.' I can take the idea that suffering can be character building, but I'd be wary of any blimpish attitude that said everyone ought to have a dose of it, like national service, to 'make a man' out of them, or because it's good for the soul. It isn't good for the soul, although you can certainly learn a great deal from it. Suffering is never welcomed but it can be embraced. And, for the Christian, one of the reasons it can be embraced is that, as St Paul is saying God can induce a sense of hope in a person that cannot be put down, or will not give up, but keeps on rising up with new vigour.

8.

Prayer – Hotline to God or number unobtainable?

Talking to God

The first thing to say about prayer is that it usually involves talking to God, putting into words something about the human relationship with God. And the second thing is that this talk usually involves asking for things: praying for health, the welfare of friends and relations, and solutions to political problems. The asking element is reinforced by the fact that church services invariably include prayers of intercession for the needs of the Church, the world and the sick, and many churches have a prayer board where people are invited to post written prayers, which typically ask God for healing, the mending of a broken relationship, or world peace.

Presumably anyone who asks God for things believes that their prayers will make a difference. For example, to pray for the healing of a sick person implies a belief that God can and will influence events. What would be the point of praying if we didn't think that God would do anything in response? But *does* God act in the world? This is a crucial question.

In the Bible there are many stories about God intervening in human events, often in a supernatural way. The Israelites, escaping from slavery in Egypt, are helped miraculously to cross the Red Sea; Lazarus, dead and stinking in the tomb, is raised back to life. Jesus takes his close disciples up a mountain where he is transfigured in such a way that he appears dazzlingly white alongside Moses and Elijah. One can't help asking whether the supernatural events described in such stories actually happened like that or whether these are stories that make a symbolic point about the power and glory of God. Today we have no experience of God acting outside the laws of nature. Scientists have identified physical and mathematical characteristics (laws) which apply over the unimaginably vast distances of the universe. If these were changed the consequences would be massive and catastrophic. So it seems certain that any creator God would not tamper with his creation. To take a simple illustration, just suppose that a person intent on suicide jumps off the Empire State Building and while passing the 50th floor changes his mind and prays, 'O God save me from death'. To answer that prayer God would have to suspend the laws of gravity but the consequence would be that everyone and everything else would fly off into space and chaotic destruction.

Christians disagree sharply about whether God acts in the world. Some believe that God simply does not act at all, for good or for bad, and given the degree of injustice and suffering in the world this view has great attractions. On the other hand some believe that God is active even in the small details of their life. There are those who pray to God to find them a parking place and believe that he often does. If a place is not available then presumably God has a good reason for frustrating the petitioner who will possibly learn by it! Wendy Cope wrote a poem called 'Strugnell's Christian Songs' in which her Christian hero, Jason Strugnell, says, 'Jesus found me a parking space, In a very convenient place. Sound the horn and praise Him!'

But this kind of belief raises an obvious and compelling objection. Why should God be concerned with the trivial matter of finding parking places when there are millions of people dying of starvation and disease, whose situation is not being ameliorated? It's an objection that I find totally convincing. It would seem blasphemous to think that divine love could be supporting the excesses of the Western life style while ignoring the plight of the Third World, and my conclusion is that either God does not act in the world or I have totally misunderstood the nature of divine activity.

That is my logical argument, but my emotional experience is different. When someone close to me is seriously ill, or when I was seriously ill myself, my prayer is one that basically asks God for a miracle. I want the person to get better, even against the biological odds, and I have to say that I think it would be a pity if that prayer became impossible because of rational objections. I certainly pray *as if* God can intervene and surprise the doctors and I'm not worried that what I am doing is inconsistent with my intellectual view, because I think it's natural and instinctive to beseech God in an extreme situation. That instinctive reaching out to God reveals a hope in the infinite love of God. I think I should not be surprised if my relationship with the divine Love is sometimes paradoxical.

If God does not act, then what?

My claim that God does not act in the world obviously needs some more comment, some 'unpacking' as they say, because it could easily be misunderstood as a pretty big step on the road to atheism. We have already seen that the most distinctive Christian belief is that the transcendent God became present in the world in the life of Jesus of Nazareth. In that life, and the story of it, we see the true nature of God as a self-giving being who demonstrates his love through service and sacrifice. And it is these upside down values – the last shall be first and the first last, whoever would save his life must lose it – that provide the true location for God's presence in the world. My claim is that God doesn't act against the laws of nature, like some sort of superman, flying in to troubleshoot problems, but that doesn't preclude a subtler presence of God in our experience. Jesus said that inasmuch as anyone shows kindness and compassion to lowliest human being, they are showing it to him. That is to say, God is present in each of us and that it is possible to see Christ in one another particularly through acts of mercy and goodness. Can it make sense, then, that God is present in the world, but active only through us? I think it can. And the Church of England liturgy recognises this: one of its summary intercession prayers virtually makes my case for me. 'Give grace to us, our families and friends, and to all our neighbours; that we may serve Christ in one another, and love as he loves us.'

Another obvious point to be made about intercessory prayer is that when a person knows they are being prayed for, they can feel buoyed up and supported, and the psychosomatic effect can be extremely healing. This happened to me when I was in hospital. I happen to live next door to one Roman Catholic Convent, the *Sacred Heart*, and opposite another, *The Holy Child*. Both communities of nuns were praying for me, which at one level I found amusing – I was benefiting from much more Roman Catholic prayer than Anglican prayer – and at another level I found comforting and reassuring. I was touched to be the subject of so much attention, so intensely and generously given.

Beyond asking

Of course, the nuns pray as a kind of work and as part of their way of life. They are doing what the Church has done over the Christian centuries, offering daily prayer to God throughout the year. There's a Latin tag that I've occasionally seen inscribed above the entrance to a monastic chapel: *orare est laborare* – to pray is to work. And above the door on the way out: *laborare est orare* – to work is to pray. It's a nice contrast, which not only suggests that the whole of life can be directed towards God, but that words need to be backed up by action. The sick person needs visiting quite as much as being named in prayer, if not more so.

So the prime purpose of the Church as an organisation is to worship God. Hence the buildings, the liturgies, the clergy, the choirs, the paintings, and all the trappings that accompany worship. The poet George Herbert said that prayer is the 'Church's banquet', a feast, a great hall with tables decked with fruit and silver bowls and candles. But I would always regard the trappings as secondary to that primary, intuitive, awesome sense that God is and is mysteriously present in the world of our ordinary experience. The essence of prayer, I think, is the response, however faltering or however bold, to that *mysterium tremendum*, that great mystery of God's being.

I started with the crude assertion that prayer is conversation with God, but conversation isn't actually a word I'd use to describe my own experience of private prayer, because I find that words can often seem inadequate and sentences run out before they have been completed. The telephone model of a 'hotline' to God doesn't work for me. Rather than being a garrulous activity, I find prayer to be at the edge of speech, and this experience of being tongue-tied may give a clue to what prayer is about at a more profound level. Being lost for words means that you can't say what you mean, you can't articulate what you want. Maybe you don't know what you want; you believe that God is there and that it's important to be in relationship with him, but beyond that your prayer is inexpressible. It is a raw gesture of reaching out for God. St Augustine in his Confessions says that the 'heart is restless until it finds its rest in God'. This seems to put very neatly what I am trying to say – that prayer is basically a matter of trying to bring one's will into line with God's will. I think of it as harmonising, getting in tune with God, and this can be a transforming experience.

Penitence – the self in context

A major key to harmonising with God is penitence, which I think is about knowing yourself and being honest about yourself before God. Lent, the period of the Church's year leading up to Easter, is of course a time when Christians think about penitence and the first day of Lent, Ash Wednesday, is a particular focus.

Last Ash Wednesday I was on holiday in Rome and despite being in the Mother City of Western Christianity I failed to find a mass to attend at a time that suited. So my reflection on penitence had to be that of a tourist rather than that of a churchgoer. Instead of a receiving the sacramental sign of an ashen cross on the forehead, which in a sense makes penitence that bit easier, or identifiable, I had only thoughts. Penitence, I thought to myself, is to do with seeing ourselves in context; to do with seeing ourselves in relation to others, and ultimately and most importantly no doubt in relation to God.

That afternoon I stood in the Colosseum. It is a massively imposing construction, awesome to the modern mind as well as the ancient. There's now a walkway over the underground cages and chambers where the wild animals were kept, where the gladiators waited and Christians were imprisoned. There's also a recently reconstructed section of arena. It's a cliché I know, but you can almost hear the roar of the crowds being entertained by violence and cruelty – the pornography of the day. I felt a personal horror at the thought of Christian martyrdom – a fact brought home to me by a large cross erected at one side of the arena. But in fact I think most people, regardless of their religious background, when they enter that arena feel a shiver down the spine as they imagine what went on here in ancient Rome and maybe experience a sense of shame at our corporate inhumanity.

That is a penitential experience – seeing ourselves in context. It strikes chords with the truth and reconciliation exercises pioneered in South Africa by Desmond Tutu, where a nation, or a party, or a people apologise and ask forgiveness for the sins of the past: Nazis of Jews, white of black, Japanese of Western Allied POW's and so on.

The next day, I stood in St Peter's contemplating Michelangelo's Pieta. This induces another kind of penitence – humility. Humility at contemplating the creative genius of another, recognising in this egotistical age that someone has achieved something I could not achieve myself. The beautiful statue was sculpted out of a single piece of stone – the conception and the technique are both mind-blowing. He did this when he was 24 years old. Dare one say it, it has a tremendous sexual energy: the woman, Mary the mother of Christ, looks about eighteen and is extremely beautiful; the figure of Christ, having been taken down from the cross and laid in her lap, still has vitality and looks about 24 years old! It speaks of a mother's sadness, but also has a kind of Romeo and Juliettish tragedy to it. My penitence here is not induced by my humility at the realisation that Christ died for me, but by the creative genius of my fellow human beings. This is an important part of seeing ourselves in context.

Entering St Peter's Square the grandeur and triumphant wealth is overwhelming. My wife, who had not been there before, commented on the irony that the founder of the Christian Faith, whom all this celebrated, had taught humility, simplicity of life, and told his followers to sell all that they had and give to the poor. No wonder, she said, that people get hold of the wrong end of the stick. And you can see her point, but there is underneath it all, literally underneath it all a sombre resonance. The Egyptian obelisk in the Square once stood in the centre of chariot circus favoured by the tyrannical Christian persecutor Nero, and the church is built pretty well on the ground plan of that circus. Underneath the high altar is the burial place and possible place of martyrdom of St Peter, Jesus' right hand man. Beneath all the baroque exuberance of Bernini, which for the suffering servant, the man of sorrows, might seem metaphorically as well as literally over the top, there was a humbling and prophetic reality which I hope many pilgrims experience. As Jesus said in Luke 9:23, 'If any want to become my disciples, let them deny themselves and take up their cross daily and follow me.' St Peter, mindful of this teaching, asked to be crucified upside down. It was his way perhaps of finally removing the guilt he felt for his betrayal of Jesus and becoming the 'rock' on which Christ's Church would be built.

But Jesus went into the *wilderness*, away from it all, away from people, away from the food and wine and roasting chestnuts, away from the buildings and social venues to contemplate his mission and his values; to contemplate God. There is of course the imaginary trip into town to the St Peter's of his day, the Temple in Jerusalem, where he is tempted to jump from the pinnacle in a bid to win converts as the flash, brash showman. But the wilderness is a lonely sojourn with God.

In the end we each need our *wilderness*, to stand alone with God, without any trappings or diversions, or artful sophistication. Penitence starts in the context of seeing ourselves in relation to others, as a self amongst many 'selves', but its zenith is the emptying of self, stripping away all the baggage of materialism, ambition, competitiveness, jealousy, and meanness that weigh us down and contribute to life being less fulfilling than it could be. This emptying of self is to do with (in an old fashioned phrase) going into the privacy of your chamber, and entering the privacy of your mind. We *think* we occupy our own minds but we never do fully; there are so many closed doors and shut passageways. Penitence before God allows us to open some of those doors and get rid of some of the contents that shame us, that we don't want any longer but most of the time can't face up to. Our prayer might be something like this: Just let me stop obsessing about this possession, or that job, or this relationship, or that failure. Just let me be free to be myself.

This freedom is achieved possibly by a conscious act of letting go, but more likely by following Jesus' recommended method of focusing on others rather than oneself. On a recent edition of the British TV dating programme, Blind Date, there was a young man who didn't think much of the young woman who had chosen him for the date or the free holiday they had had together in Scotland. He criticised his date, the hotel, the Scottish scenery and thought them all boring, unattractive and not good enough for him. Cilla Black, the hostess of this most theological of programmes, then said to him, 'Has it ever occurred to you, Chuck, that you're no great shakes yourself?' He was stunned and the audience whistled and applauded Cilla for minutes.

This contemporary parable might equally well apply to prayer. The prayer that harmonises with God is the one in which you see your life in the context of others and not with you at the centre of the universe. It harmonises with God because in the Christian view God's own nature is one which is totally self-giving as we see exemplified in Jesus Christ who took the form of a servant and revealed his divinity in the very act of giving his life for others.

Prayer as poetry

So if there is an intrinsic ambiguity to prayer – talking to God on the one hand and being reduced to a stunned silence on the other – what does this have to say about written prayers and public worship? Are they at the shallow end of prayer and is silence superior? They can certainly be banal but at their best they can also be poetic. One only has to think of the resonance and rhythm of the Book of Common Prayer where the beauty of language somehow transcends rational analysis. I certainly don't want to underestimate words in the prayerful search for God and I find that many classic prayers express in words what you might call the beauty of holiness. Just consider these lines from the Prayer Book: 'O God, forasmuch as without thee we are not able to please thee'; 'O God, the protector of all who put their trust in thee'; 'Stir up, we beseech thee O Lord, the wills of thy faithful people'; 'create and make in us new and contrite hearts.' This is poetical language capable of heightening the spiritual experience.

The poet Ted Hughes says that poetry comes from the place of the ultimate suffering and decision in us. I think he means that it comes from deep inside our experience and speaks of what is vitally important to us. I think prayer comes from the same place. It can't always be transparently clear what it means or is saying; it is something that searches for meaning and understanding. It is an attempt to put ourselves in touch with the Divine. If you write a poem rather than a note, or a memo, or a letter, it means you have thought very carefully about your subject with a great deal of attention. That is why people in love write poems to their beloved, because they are giving that person all the attention they can muster. So it is with prayer: prayer is a special way of concentrating on God, attending to God, and if enough people attend to God in that way, then it will make a difference.

Some well-loved prayers, like poems, stick in the memory and form a model for what prayer can be. The Lord's Prayer is an obvious example, but so would be the Prayer of St Francis of Assisi. 'Lord, make me an instrument of your peace; where there is hatred, let me sow love; where there is injury, pardon ...'

One of the finest prayer/poems I know was written by John Donne in the 17th century and is very popular at funerals and memorial services because it manages to capture a wonderful vision of heaven.

'Bring us, O Lord God, at our last awakening, into the house and gate of heaven, to enter into that gate and dwell in that house, where there shall be no darkness nor dazzling, but one equal light; no noise nor silence, but one equal music; no fears nor hopes, but one equal possession; no ends nor beginnings, but one equal eternity; in the habitation of thy glory and dominion, world without end. Amen.'

Perhaps it is no accident that John Donne was a prolific writer of love poems before he became a preacher and a writer of religious poetry!

Communal Prayer

I am always fascinated and encouraged how often, in our secular society, a politician or public figure, interviewed on TV after a public tragedy, will say that the victims and relatives are 'in our thoughts and prayers'. I am encouraged that it can be so easily and naturally assumed that we have this in common and I guess it's both because the instinct of prayer runs deep but also that prayer is a common activity to people of different faiths and therefore can cross those boundaries. It is a way of expressing the degree of our concern, and somehow referring that concern beyond the inadequate human response to a higher plane, to God. In the face of extreme circumstances, in which you feel helpless or impotent, this at least is something that you can *do* and I think at times of national crisis or national mourning, just as at times of personal crisis, people from a wide spectrum of faith and doubt are drawn together to pray. This was evident before and during the war with Iraq in which vigils for peace drew people who do not usually worship together. They were joined by a common bond of wanting peace and abominating violence and would have reinforced each other's views through that common activity.

Interestingly this reflects what happens generally when Christians meet to pray together. I have mainly discussed personal prayer, but corporate prayer is an essential part of Christian identity because it is very hard to be a Christian on your own. Not only does meeting together help provide communal identity and define the community's relation to God, it is also a corporate act in which common beliefs are articulated and reinforced. Rather than being in any way Big Brotherish, this seems to me the most natural and creative way of preserving tradition by telling the Christian story over and over again. In fact it is generally accepted that the early traditions of Christianity, before they were written down in the New Testament, were preserved in exactly that way by their constant re-telling in worship. One of the best examples is the use of Paul's description of the last supper in his first letter to the Corinthians as a prayer in every communion service or mass. This narrative of the Last Supper is the centrepiece of the Thanksgiving Prayer for the body and blood of Christ, and in that context turns from historical account into a prayerful evocation not only of Christ's sacrifice but also the Church's hope in the eternal future, for, as St Paul says, by eating the bread and drinking the wine 'you proclaim the Lord's death until he comes'.

The prayers of public worship are naturally full of ideas about God and what Christians believe. Anyone wanting to know what Christianity is about would get a very good idea from listening to the whole of the Thanksgiving Prayer at the Eucharist because in addition to the Last Supper, it includes the story of salvation from the creation to the resurrection and ascension of Jesus.

Prayer in this context is a way of holding the faith of the Church together. It is also why I said at the beginning that I am liturgically conservative, because the liturgy of the Church provides a good framework for belief that I like to be anchored in. I appreciate the fact that it is ancient and traditional and less susceptible to the whim and occasional manipulation of unstructured prayer.

9.
Out of this world

In what I have said so far, I realise I have assumed that there is a gulf that has to be bridged between what you might call 'godly' values and what you might call 'worldly' values. The duality between spirit and flesh or between Heaven and Earth is obviously a part of Christianity's vocabulary. Besides the incarnation is precisely about God bridging that gap. I don't know how much this presents a problem to people today or to what degree it is a barrier to faith for the liberal mind, but I thought it worth considering.

There's an old joke about a vicar being too heavenly minded to be of any earthly use. It supports a popular image of priests as impractical starry-eyed idealists with their minds on higher things and spotlights one of the great dilemmas of Christianity: how to live in the world and yet be spiritual. This ambivalence about the world goes back to the New Testament where Jesus says that his kingdom is not of this world and tells his followers that they do not belong to the world and can expect to be hated by it. It's a view strongly backed by St Paul who says that the things of the world, particularly the pleasures of the flesh, are quite opposite to the spiritual values that Jesus reveals. He even says that he never wishes to boast of anything except the cross of our Lord Jesus Christ, by which 'the world has been crucified to me, and I to the world.'

Of course, for the people of the New Testament the world meant something very different from what it does to us. For them it was the Roman Empire around the Mediterranean Sea and particularly the hostile attitude that they encountered towards the growing Christian religion. It was this political order that cruelly persecuted Christianity and mocked the spiritual values that Paul identified as love, joy, peace, kindness, generosity, and self-control. So in the face of animosity and persecution it must have been tempting to vilify the world and to try to live apart from it. Also there was a clear expectation amongst the first

Christians, evident again in the writing of St Paul, that the world was going to end in their lifetime. They believed that Jesus Christ would return in glory to judge the world and establish God's rule. All earthly politics and power would come to an end so, as St Paul said to the Christians at Corinth, what was the point even of getting married, buying a house, and trying to set yourself up for the future? Normal life was about to end and Christians ought to spend their lives prayerfully waiting for God's kingdom to come. But it didn't come. Jesus didn't return to overturn the worldly powers and Christianity had to make its way in a frequently hostile environment.

But in all this there's a paradox. The Jesus who said that his kingdom was not of this world is also the one who bothered to come into the world. As St John says, 'God so loved the world that he gave his only begotten son'. Rather than disdain the world God entered the mess of everyday life in the impoverished circumstances of a stable in Bethlehem where he was greeted by uneducated, rough shepherds who represented a kind of raw, unsophisticated and not very religious humanity.

This paradox has run throughout Christian history and is seen in the various attitudes that Christians have had to the world. On the non-worldly side there is the monastic movement in which Christians have lived a life of prayer in set-apart communities that espouse the values of poverty, chastity and obedience. And there have been a variety of smaller world-renouncing groups, such as the Anabaptists of the Reformation who deliberately set themselves apart in their theology and lifestyle. Under Oliver Cromwell's Protectorate in England the theatre and the celebration of Christmas were banned! Such other worldliness is ludicrous and excessive, but at its best the self-denial of Christians can be pro-phetic, challenging both other Christians and non-Christians to think through their spiritual and moral priorities and to find a lifestyle that respects Christ's teaching and example. At its worst it can lead to the kind of cultic exclusivity which under fanatical and paranoid leadership can be positively dangerous, such as happened in Waco with the Branch Davidians under the leadership of David Kureishi.

In the early part of the fourth century the Emperor Constantine made Chris-tianity the official religion of the Roman Empire. Almost at a stroke Christianity was changed from a persecuted religion to one that was officially promoted. Instead of being against it, the 'world' was now potentially on its side. So on the worldly side of the paradox we find that Christianity, where it has been suc-cessful in promoting its message, has sometimes become institutionalised and established as part of the social fabric. This happened in England with Bishops in Parliament and a role for the Church in solemnising the great symbolic moments of national life – coronations, royal weddings and funerals. The association of Church and State can lead to accusations of compromise – rendering to Caesar what rightfully belongs to God. Although it can be argued that the most effective way to put the spiritual and moral insights of Christianity into practice is to work within the structures of society, not outside them. The danger for established Christianity is of course that its representatives can develop a taste for wealth and power that in turn blunts their capacity for spiritual and prophetic leadership. This happened notoriously with the Papacy in late 15th century Italy, when the Borgia popes committed murder and fornication with mafialike unscrupulousness in their search for political power and pleasure.

For my own part this tension between the world and denial of the world presents me with a difficulty especially at the level of my image as a priest. A priest loses credibility if he or she is seen to too worldly, and gains credibility by being perceived as holy and spiritual. Yet I regard my Christianity as unashamedly world affirming. I even think of myself more as a secular person than a religious one and I don't think you have to be especially religious to know God, although the collective experience of religion can help. I locate my religion in the middle of the society I belong to, which for all its faults, I find positive and stimulating. I want my faith to embrace it, not to hide away from it in a cul-de-sac, pretending that it doesn't exist. The idea that you can cut yourself off from 'the world' must be an illusion anyway, since we are human and wherever we run to our experience is always in the world. In any case I find the renunciation of worldly things unattractive and I want to enjoy what the world has to offer, as given by God, and not feel guilty about it. It seems to me that this approach is supported by the story of Jesus, who clearly enjoyed the pleasures of an active social life, as borne out by the fact that he was regularly criticised for going to the parties thrown by publicans and sinners. He didn't want to spoil a pleasant Saturday afternoon walk by allowing the law against working on the Sabbath to stop him picking an ear of corn and eating it. And he certainly wasn't going to allow the same law to stop him healing a man with a withered hand on the Sabbath day. Life is more important than religion! As he said at the time, the Sabbath was made for man not man for the Sabbath.

But there has to be something distinctive about being and living as a Christian which makes a difference, otherwise why bother? So however much I want to affirm the society I belong to I have to recognise that there is a critique of the world innate to Christian theology, which could be summed up as: love versus selfishness. This is really what lies behind the world/not-of-the-world distinction. It's the body and soul thing, the flesh and the spirit, the idea that the self-centred survival instinct, the basic biological force that sustains life on this beautiful blue-green planet, must be tempered with a bit of love, kindness and ungrabbing contentment if it's going to be worthwhile. A life of personal self-discipline and tireless attention to other people is the mark of holiness, and therefore is a sense of unworldliness. But all of this is to anticipate the next chapter about the nature of Christian morality and Jesus' surprising and disturbing teaching that whoever would save their life must lose it, and his question asking what profit there is in gaining the whole world if you lose your soul.

10.
Do you need God to be good?

Do you need God to be good? Judging by some of the prayers of the Church of England you definitely do. For example, the collect for the First Sunday after Trinity says to God, 'because through the weakness of our mortal nature we can do no good thing without you, grant us the help of your grace', and the collect for the Nineteenth Sunday after Trinity begins, 'O God, forasmuch as without you we are not able to please you'. This suggests that all goodness comes from God and that acts of goodness, whether we know it or not, derive from God. This is an attractive and helpful idea to me as a Christian because I understand my life in relation to the God who created me, but for the humanist, who doesn't accept the existence of God, it is obviously ludicrous, and even offensive. The humanist would point out that there are many honest, neighbourly people who have no religious faith at all, and that Christian history isn't exactly festooned with lives that are obviously better than others. So religion should not be seen as the only source of morality, because how we behave may be influenced by what we think is naturally or self-evidently right or by practical strategies for living together peacefully as a social group.

Nevertheless Christianity has a very distinctive moral quality about it, which I think depends on two things: first the belief that self-giving love is the fundamental moral principle, and secondly that it holds before us a compellingly impressive life, Jesus, which we also believe was a divine life. Christian ethics ask us to think about the kind of person Jesus was and in doing so to think about God. How would Christ have behaved in this or that situation, what would he have had to say to us today? There are memorable teachings such as, blessed are the peace makers, and the requirement to go the extra mile, but he also saw the good in everyone, however socially resented or despised they were. His words and actions seem perfectly matched.

What is the essence of Jesus' moral teaching?

We get a major clue to this in the Sermon on the Mount where, in a series of illustrations, he elaborates what he means when he says that he came to fulfil the Jewish law. He suggests that one needs to look behind practical rules in order to discover their moral essence. For example, behind murder lies the motive of anger and insulting disregard for others; behind adultery lies a self-indulgent lust that treats others as objects. Obviously in the eyes of the law anger and lust are not crimes and are not punishable as such, nor is Christ suggesting that they should be. He recognised that anger and lust are natural emotions that each of us experiences from time to time, and that even though their moral character might be of the same essence as murder and adultery, self-control is an over-riding virtue. But it is clear that Jesus' morality is concerned as much with motivation as with deed, because he believes that the root of wrongdoing lies in people's attitude of mind.

This is also illustrated by his loathing of hypocrisy and false piety, objecting to those who make a show of praying on the street corner, or publicly giving alms, or disfiguring their faces to show that they are fasting. It is important to practice what you preach and to be unostentatious and humble, otherwise a person's morality becomes no more than a status symbol, a self-aggrandising projection of social image. He said that not everyone who says, 'Lord, Lord,' will enter the kingdom of heaven, but only the one who does the will of my Father in heaven.

On the practical side we see Jesus' morality exemplified in his social conscience as he preaches good news to the poor, release to the captives, recovery of sight to the blind, and freedom for the oppressed. He lives this out in such events as healing on the Sabbath, where the welfare of the sufferer is put before religious observance, and in the way he restores dignity to social outcasts such as Zacchaeus the Jericho tax collector with whom he pointedly chose to dine rather than with the religious leaders. There is also evidence of a radical social morality in the value he gives to women in a society that generally held them in low esteem. He advocated better terms for women in divorce settlements, saved a woman from being stoned to death for adultery, and allowed a woman publicly to anoint his feet and wipe them with her hair.

If you boil down Jesus' moral agenda you find that he is greatly concerned with the harmful effect that wealth and violence can have on morality, that he has little to say about sex and power (despite the Christian obsession with these things), and that he is massively in favour of forgiveness, reconciliation and the love of neighbour. In fact what we get from Jesus' teachings and life-style is a theory of ethics rather than an applied system or moral rulebook. He doesn't provide easy answers to moral dilemmas, but instead gives an overarching principle for making moral decisions, a basic moral standard – namely, to establish what would be the most selflessly loving action in any particular situation.

He's a dreamer and a utopian with a vision of purity and perfection. At the beginning of the Sermon on the Mount he says, 'Blessed are the pure in heart' and at the end he concludes, 'be perfect as your heavenly Father is perfect' – an obvious counsel of perfection which others might call reckless idealism. He speaks of loving your enemies and turning the other cheek. These famous sayings are metaphors for this reckless idealism, not necessarily to be taken literally. Of course there will be occasions when it is right physically to go out of your way to help someone and occasions when it will be right to show complete passivity in the face of aggression, but not always. Would one say to the terrorist, please bomb our shopping centre again or expect a battered wife to take a second beating? Of course not; but that argument doesn't neutralise the force of Christ's idealism, which is intended not to induce moral paralysis by asking too much, but to push us to the limits of moral self-giving.

My use of the word 'reckless' carries with it the sense of 'risky', and Jesus is saying that you must take the risk of love, which is also a risk that you might get hurt. That, I think, is what is meant by turning the other cheek – making oneself vulnerable in the quest for goodness.

How can we best illustrate the vulnerability of love? Perhaps by the model of parenthood in which a mother or father is driven instinctively to guard their child whatever the physical or financial risk to themselves. Or perhaps by the lover who at the outset of a relationship must risk the humiliation of rejection – nothing ventured, nothing gained – and in the course of mature relationship must often make sacrifices by putting personal interests second. This is what is so brilliantly captured in the words of the Christian marriage service: for better for worse, for richer for poorer, in sickness and in health. But this ideal doesn't just apply to marriage and parenthood – it applies to any relationship whether intimate or professional, political or international. It is much easier to see how the vulnerability of love works at the personal level, but in fact it can be translated to the large-scale political level too. The demise of apartheid in South Africa would be an example, or the release of a poor country from debt by a rich country would be another. It is possible, but doesn't happen often.

Jesus' morality from another angle

When the Royal Shakespeare Company produced the Mystery Plays for the London stage in the mid 1990s, the scriptwriter, Edward Kemp, found that the actors were pretty unfamiliar with religion and hadn't much understanding of what made Jesus tick. So he held a workshop to help them get a handle on it. He decided they needed to identify the dramatic tensions in the story. Part of this was to understand its moral teaching. So they drew up a list of Jesus' concerns in the form of oppositions which came out like this:

> altruism versus selfishness
> responsibility versus irresponsibility
> community versus individualism
> spiritual versus material values
> harmonious nature versus man's abuse of creation.

These were the issues, they decided, that Jesus was addressing and he tried to draw a society away from the latter towards the former in each case. The actors said they thought the issues that were current for Jesus' time still seemed current now and this would help them perform with greater energy and conviction. What made the story dramatic was the fact that Jesus needed to say these things in the first place and that his society felt it necessary to kill him for saying them, and then that others felt his message sufficiently important to promote it, even at the cost of their own lives. 'This seemed like a story worth telling,' said Kemp, 'independently of whether we could commit to particular beliefs about the man's divinity.'

Idealism in practice

The problem of how to apply Christian ideals in practice is the subject of continuous debate. My Dictionary of Christian Ethics runs to 700 pages and covers issues ranging from government to war, sexuality to divorce, genetic engineering to euthanasia, and poverty to wealth. On all of these questions there are Christians who hold different or opposite views, even though they have started from the same basic texts and principles. The problem is that what a person believes is right depends on how they interpret Scripture, what weight they give to traditional Christian teaching, and indeed which part of the world they come from, since local customs and traditions have great influence. There are Christians who oppose abortion in all cases and those who do not; Christians who are pacifists and those who are not; Christians who believe in the cancellation of Third World debt and those who do not. Basically there is rarely a clear cut, generally agreed, Christian teaching on a particular moral question, which can be particularly frustrating to those who want Church leaders to 'speak out'. It is not surprising that the title of the popular radio programme on ethics, The Moral Maze, has caught on as a general description of the difficult moral choices that face modern society.

Moral certainty or relativism?

The fact that Christians sometimes disagree over moral issues can lead to insecurity and loss of confidence amongst them. It's the same problem that we noted earlier in relation to the Bible about the desire for clear cut certainties of faith. You might expect God as the ultimate moral authority to provide unequivocal moral laws such as the Ten Commandments. There ought, you might think, to be little room for debate for those who receive their guidance from God. Yet, in practice even the Church itself, consulting the sacred texts and seeking guidance from the Holy Spirit through prayer, finds it difficult to be definitive on issues such as whether divorced persons should remarry in church, whether practising homosexuals should be ordained, or whether bombing suspected terrorist bases is consistent with the theory of a just war.

The reality is that Christians have to make moral judgements based on God given principles. You might say that instead of following a given set of rules, the Christian has to act according to conscience and in personal relationship with God. This is broadly the position I take myself. To be more specific I would say that there is one overarching God-given principle, self-giving love, and that this is the model for all moral action. It is the principle of loving attention to others and actually constitutes a high view of moral authority based on the teaching of Jesus. But the fact that the application of the principle sometimes results in different outcomes can lead to the criticism that it's a liberal approach in which 'anything goes' – a form of relativism or compromise. I don't accept that because self-giving love isn't relative; it doesn't vary from one society to another; it seems to me a universal principle that human beings can understand instinctively. It has to do with compassion, kindness and consideration, and with putting yourself into someone else's shoes. If you accept that Jesus Christ, the Son of God, exemplifies this kind of love most fully, then you would be likely to agree that the moral action that follows has divine authority.

There is of course much about ethics that is relative; it is a simple fact that has to be faced. In the Bible itself there are cultural differences such as the fact that Kings David and Solomon have many wives but Jesus advocates that a man should have only one wife. In the sixteenth century it was thought good to burn heretics at the stake for the sake of their immortal souls, now it would seem a moral outrage. I think it's important to recognise that the interpretation of morality changes and develops in the same way as doctrine changes and develops. For Christians it starts from first principles and is a continuous process of refinement, usually tending towards improvement but sometimes, of course, taking a retrograde step.

Christian Action

Christianity is, then, an ethical religion. Believing in God has implications for how a person ought to behave and the quality both of an individual's and the Church's faith is judged by how they act. My favourite summary of this is St Francis of Assisi's instruction to his Brothers when he sent them out into the Italian countryside on a mission at the beginning of the thirteenth century, 'Preach the Gospel everywhere, if necessary using words'. Christian action should be the natural by-product of Christian faith and Christianity's greatest advertisement.

This came home to me when Desmond Tutu visited Oxford for a week in 1996 and I had the privilege of accompanying him for the whole of that time. Walking through the streets people would rush up to him, shake him by the hand, and thank him for all that he had done in South Africa. Christianity is at its strongest when it is political and kicking against the political status quo, and weakest when it is propping up the system. Who speaks up for the poor, the marginalized, and the discriminated against? Who speaks against big business, the social division of wealth? His charisma was that he had conspicuously put his faith into practice, preaching with action as much as with words. This made his brand of Christianity, which was about reconciliation and breaking down the barriers of race, immensely compelling, even to people who otherwise had little fascination for religion.

When we went into Oxford prison (which was at that time still a working prison), he met a group of inmates and his opening remark to them was, 'Jesus loves you; he loves every one of you'. They looked at him open-mouthed as if he was mad. Very few people would have got away with it, but he held their attention and was soon chatting easily with the group, I think because, even though he might have seemed an eccentric black man in a purple shirt, he obviously cared for them as people and understood their situation.

Wealth, sex, and power

There used to be a restaurant on the ground floor of the Church of England Headquarters, Church House, Westminster, where the staff and General Synod members liked to eat. It was an Italian restaurant called the *Vitello D'Oro*, the golden calf. I don't know whether it was a coincidence or whether the franchisee was poking fun at the Christians upstairs by naming his restaurant after the most famous false God of the Old Testament.

The making of a golden calf was in breach of the first and second commandments of YHWH: You shall have no other gods but me, and that you shall not make any graven image, nor the likeness of anything that is in heaven above or in the earth beneath ... for I the Lord your God am a jealous God. It was also a symbol of materialism. They made it of precious metal melted down from their prized jewellery, earrings and necklaces. You might say how sacrificial of them to give up their personal possessions to make their god, but the fact remained it was a god made of possessions.

At the opposite pole to this superstitious religion, the New Testament offers the spiritual religion of St Paul's 'fruits of the Spirit'. The antithesis brings into focus again the clash between the materialism of our basic instincts and the self-sacrificial love of the Christian vision. The one is critiqued by the other; love constantly asks questions of human acquisitiveness, self-aggrandisement and motivation.

To clarify my thoughts I thought it might be helpful to make a list of false gods and immediately came up with the old formula of 'Wealth, Sex and Power', often seen on billboards outside churches advertising sermons on morality. The passer by has more than a hunch that the sermons won't actually be recommending these alluring seductions, but it looks more exciting than 'Poverty, Chastity and Obedience'. The fight will be on between moral aspiration and basic instincts.

You could bundle them all together under the false god of 'materialism', but materialism by itself simply won't do. We are all material and we live in a material world which God made and chose to become material in. Also, one of the insights of the Bible is that God is being; the YHWH whom Moses encountered on the mountain claimed to be 'I am'. When Moses asked God his name at the Burning Bush, God replied, 'I AM WHO I AM' (Exodus 3). It might be argued from this that all being is in God and that all the spiritual qualities admired by St Paul are only possible through the medium of the material – our bodies and minds. So the making of false gods is about *how* we use the material, not that the material exists, hence Paul's insight that the *love* of money is the root of all evil.

Christianity certainly offers a radical critique of wealth. Jesus says that you can't serve God and Mammon. In Luke 18:22 he advises the rich young man who wants to be a disciple to sell all that he has and give the money to the poor. And most famously he says that it's easier for a camel to go through the eye of needle than for a rich person to enter the kingdom of heaven. In our own culture we see the almost religious idolisation of wealth in the way we make icons out of film stars, footballers, and models, celebrating their life style in newspapers and glossy magazines and hankering after it. Wealth is seen as a virtue and flaunted in the face of poverty.

How to be rich and a Christian presents a dilemma, but not for everyone. Some Christians in North America have promoted the idea of 'prosperity' theology, which says that God rewards those who have faith with material prosperity. I find that theologically and morally a totally unacceptable idea and on a par with the 'parking meter' theology I mentioned in the chapter on prayer. Most Christians will be mindful of what has been called Jesus' 'bias to the poor', which in the 1970s and 1980s became a slogan for 'liberation theology', the movement that rightly emphasised the social implications of Christianity, especially for the Third World. However, I do not believe that the gospel message is anti-wealth *per se*. Jesus seemed to enjoy the company of the wealthy and to a large degree depended on their support for a ministry that otherwise had no funding.

What he did emphasise, I think, is the importance of contentment, of knowing that enough is enough. This was based on a sense of divine providence. One shouldn't be worrying about accumulating treasures on earth. Consider the lilies of the field, which neither toil nor spin yet are dressed more beautifully than Solomon in all his glory. This contentment with enough, and not always demanding more, is what being satisfied means and I always regard satisfaction as a Christian virtue. This argument clearly extends into the whole area of ecology and what is called 'Green Theology'. From the Christian point of view, our responsibility for how we use the resources of the planet is usually based on the stories of creation in Genesis – that we are stewards of the world God has given us and have a duty to honour it – but Jesus' affirmation of the material, his prophetic call for justice for the poor, and his advocacy of contentment with enough, are just as significant.

To many people's surprise Jesus doesn't have much to say about sex. Matthew avers that Jesus was conceived without sexual intercourse, and the gospels imply that he never married, but Jesus only makes two or three allusions to sexual morality. It's really St Paul who gets Christians so hung up about it with his advice to the Corinthians (given in the light of his expectation of the imminent end of the world) not to marry, and his periodic reprimands about various improprieties. In reality we all know that if the sex drives were less strong than they are, the human race simply wouldn't survive for salvation to take its course. In a sense then: no sex, no salvation!

Our society has made a false god of sex by exploiting the erotic as the principal tool of advertising and the primary diet of entertainment and allowing the easy availability of pornography. You might say that as a liberal none of this should worry me, but liberalism is a disposition not an absolute. It works within a framework, be it humanist or religious. The Christian liberal will apply a Christian critique to sexual ethics, which derives from Jesus' respect of persons and as far as possible will be liberating rather than repressive. It doesn't exclude pleasure and pleasure certainly shouldn't be added to any list of false gods because Christianity isn't in principle kill joy and shouldn't be guilt inducing. God gave us life and God gave us pleasure to be enjoyed.

As for power, we all have it, whether it's physical strength, power of personality, or the power given to our role in society: parent, manager, officer, priest, Member of Parliament. Even the so-called disempowered (the unemployed, old people on low incomes, the socially marginalized) are not totally without it. Personal power can be extended through money (spending power), clothes (power dressing), cars (power symbols) and weapons (fire power, nuclear power). For obvious reasons the survival instinct drives us to want to be powerful rather than weak, but the love of power can get out of hand, as in the case of the control-freak or the tyrant. Jesus' message stands in critical opposition to the desire for power. In the Sermon on the Mount he said, do not resist an evildoer. But if anyone strikes you on the right cheek, turn the other also. This was an attitude he modelled at his own trial when, to the amazement of Pilate, he remained silent in the face of false accusations from the chief priests and elders. Also in Matthew there is the famous occasion when his opponents tried to trap him with the question whether it was lawful to pay taxes to the Emperor and he replied, 'Render to Caesar the things that are Caesar's and to God the things that are God's'. This has usually been taken to suggest that he was happy to keep the temporal and the spiritual in separate compartments, although there can be no doubt that his teaching had massive social and political implications. In fact he almost certainly had a strong eschatological sense that the end of the world order was at hand, so what did Rome matter? There was a new power about to break in, a spiritual power, when people would see the 'Son of Man coming in clouds with great power and glory'.

In the contemporary world riven by terrorism, civil and tribal wars, and the massive division between the richest and the poorest nations, the issue of power and how to use it is such a fundamental challenge to humanity that I think the particular 'flavour' of one's Christianity in approaching it is irrelevant. Terror is evil, but is it most effectively countered by military campaigns against nations? If you identify a tyrannical dictator in possession of weapons of mass destruction should you use pre-emptive military force to disarm him? How much collateral damage and death to innocent civilians is justifiable in achieving your military goal? Is the condition of life for those living under the dictatorship so terrible that they would welcome intervention from outside, even at the cost of losing lives?

Although Christians disagree on the ethics of war, within a range from complete pacifism to active military service, there can be little doubt that the Christian moral vision always looks towards peace and reconciliation. Blessed are the peacemakers, for they shall be called children of God. And when Christianity is in prophetic mode, it needs to speak unequivocally because the prophet must shock his hearers into action and too much equivocation will only cloud the vision. The prophet asks questions, but does not necessarily provide the answers. The prophet holds the politician to moral account and will be a thorn in the side of anyone who wants to declare war, since war is always a gruesome and traumatic business usually creating as many problems as it solves. Modern high tech war is no exception. It might be presented as a clean and exact science with 'precision bombing', but it generates massive collateral suffering and long term psychological trauma. The Christian prophet will hold up the life of Christ as an example and will also ask what changes can or should be made in the world to rectify the injustices that lead desperate people to violence. It may be that ultimately the political case for war is seen to be overwhelming, but in the process of reaching that political decision it is essential that the call to peace has been heard with its full prophetic force.

Seeing ethics close up

At this point it is appropriate to mention what seems to me another important Christian moral insight: the way in which Jesus deals with moral issues at the personal and individual level rather than at a distance in a general, philosophical way. This stems from the loving attention he shows to people, concentrating on their needs as if they were the only person that mattered. He didn't for example address slavery or Roman politics, but dealt with personal situations such as the 'Woman taken in Adultery' whom he protected from those who wanted to stone her (John 8), Jairus, whose daughter was dying (Mark 5), and the lawyer to whom he told the story of the 'Good Samaritan' (Luke 10).

I'm reminded of the advertisement technique that starts off with a camera shot of the world from space, and then closes in first on a country, then a city, then a house, and then a kitchen or a bedroom within the house. The technique puts the personal need in the context of global availability. And if you take it as an analogy for ethics it suggests that a moral problem is only adequately identified when we see through the broad, general view to a particular circumstance, because the broad and general view can easily hide the intimacy of suffering. The war masks the individual burning to death and all the agony of that, the flood masks the agony of the individual drowning or looking on the sight of their devastated home. In war or the contemplation of war it is unfortunately too easy to lose sight of personal horror and suffering because we are distanced from it by technology and statistics. If we had to take a sword and thrust it into another man in one to one conflict then perhaps we would recoil. Moral judgement requires us to think about how an action affects an individual person.

When she appeared on *Parkinson* on TV, Kate Adie was asked to describe what it was like to be a war reporter and she responded by telling two stories that had the audience rapt. In Sarajevo after the bombing she visited a woman who was vacuum cleaning the dust from a room that had no walls. And in Northern Ireland at Christmas she visited a house where there had been shooting and she entered a room to find a little boy who said, 'My daddy, my daddy', and slumped beneath the Christmas tree was a dead man. These stories of resilience and intimate suffering needed no explanation, because in a very intimate way they illustrate the pity of war.

In the first 90 years of the 20th century, from 1900 to 1989 it is reckoned that 100 people died every hour in war or from its side effects. Obviously in practice there were concentrations of death as in the two world wars. But the frightening statistic is that on average 100 died every hour for 90 years and amongst those were millions of civilians, women and children. Many will have died horrendously from starvation, in camps, in bombing raids, in the atomic infernos of Hiroshima and Nagasaki, or as a result of violent and perverted torture. Generally their stories are not known, but a moral response requires that at least some of them should be known. Only the close up intimate account is likely to influence the larger political decisions.

That is perhaps why the murder of the two girls from Soham in Cambridge-shire, mentioned in Chapter Three, so affected the public mood. Events such as these, looked at through the magnifying glass of the media, bring home to us the potential for human depravity. We recoil from it not simply in self-right-eous indignation, but because we recognise that we are all human and that our potential for goodness is balanced by our potential for evil. It is frightening and indignation is partly a corporate goading of ourselves to be better, more loving, more responsible. That is one of the reasons why people go to church, I suspect: to find the spiritual resources that will help us to be better, more loving, more responsible people.

11.
A few hot potatoes

At the end of this book I argue that the Church needs to clear the decks of the issues that have dominated its internal agenda for the past 20 years in order to make space for the wider concerns and needs of society. What I have in mind are those hot potatoes that repeatedly hijack church discussions such as homosexuality, other faiths, women's ministry, and biblical interpretation. I am not saying that these are insignificant questions. It is simply that the Church has been unable to resolve them, so they are always hanging around. They are important issues of justice that touch our strongest emotions and self-identity, several hitting the raw nerve of our sexual insecurities.

I have a strong sense that we need now to move forward with a decisive step, rather than relying on gradual change. Of course gradual change is more comfortable since it tends not to turn life upside down and is more the way of gentleness and diplomacy. But it can clog up the works.

I think the long debate about the remarriage of divorced people in church illustrates the problem. The Church of England has just officially accepted this, but not without years of prevarication. Obviously the Church has always wanted to uphold the ideal of Christian marriage, part of which is lifelong commitment, but it also recognises that people make mistakes, relationships go wrong, and there has to be an opportunity for forgiveness and a new start. Twenty years ago in the Church of England, the majority view was that remarriage in church constituted a moral compromise with social trends. Now the Church has approved the practice because the social gap had widened so much that it was losing touch with what is socially acceptable. That suggests to me that the Church should be careful not to automatically assume that society is wrong and ethically less sophisticated than the Church.

The model is there in the New Testament. Jesus brought his theological critique to a particular society. Judaism under Roman occupation in first century Palestine does not represent a universal society. Therefore you have to tease out the essential message of Christianity and apply it to successive societies. Politics and society have a life of their own and there must be a continuous dialogue between Christianity and society in which Christianity doesn't bury its head in the sand, but tries to bring out the best in society by affirming what is good and criticising what is bad. Hence Jesus' image of yeast and salt. The gospel is like the small pinch of yeast that leavens the whole lump of dough and makes the bread rise or like the pinch of salt added to your cooking which brings out the flavour of the whole dish.

But what are we to do about the hot potatoes, where opposing views fall into the irresistible force and immovable object category? Is homosexuality a natural aspect of sexuality to be celebrated or a deviancy condemned by the Bible? Is Christianity the only route to God or one of many? Are women priests and women bishops ruled out by the Bible? Does the Bible provide us with rules and guidance direct from God, or is it the story of the human search for God on which Christians can build both their Church and spirituality?

If we were to follow the precedent of the remarriage-of-divorced-people-in-church case, then the ethical judgement of our own society (and large parts of the Church) would encourage a very open view on all of those points. So let's take each one in turn.

Homosexuality

The Bible has very little to say about homosexuality. In fact it has very little to say about sexuality in general, as we noted in the chapter on ethics. But there are verses that condemn homosexuality such as Leviticus 18:22 where it is described as an 'abomination' and Romans 1:26 where it is called 'unnatural'. These inform the moral debate but, as judgements from an ancient culture, have to stand alongside modern medical and psychological knowledge as well as contemporary Christian understandings of the purpose of relationship. It was interesting, for example, that the Book of Common Prayer saw the first purpose of marriage as procreation, whereas the modern wedding service gives priority to friendship. This subtle shift of balance recognises that sex has much wider purposes than the begetting of children.

Where the Church has claimed that homosexuality is wrong, it has been careful to distinguish sexual orientation from same gender sexual acts – it's OK to be gay so long as you don't have gay sex. But it's a halfway house; a bit mealy mouthed and seems to be hiding from the real issue. It's also partly a generation thing: most people under 30 don't see being gay or lesbian as a problem. It's simply not an issue. Live and let live. Furthermore, although newspapers and films might suggest we are a voyeuristic society, most of us don't want to know what goes on in our neighbour's or our priest's bedroom. When people parade their sexuality in public, canoodling and touching, we find it embarrassing or inappropriate. Actual sex between couples should be private. It may be nice when idealised on screen, but in reality, however delightful, it can be a clumsy and not very interesting or compelling spectacle.

What Christianity does best is to teach about quality of *relationship* – commitment, self-giving, and long-suffering. St Paul's great chapter on love, 1 Corinthians 13, describes it brilliantly. Love is patient, kind, not envious or boastful and rejoices in the truth. Get the quality of relationship right and it is likely that morality will flow like a never-ending stream.

Of course, the final sticking point on the issue of homosexuality for the Church is the ordination of practising homosexuals. The fact is most bishops are ordaining homosexuals but daren't admit it for fear of causing schism in the Church and because the clash between social reality and a residual attachment to Biblical literalism that is hard to shake off.

The Lambeth Conference (of Anglican Bishops from all over the world) of 1998, where there was a clash between pre-critical and post-critical attitudes to the Bible, was very divided on the issue of sexuality. The conference formulated a statement that 'abstinence is right for those not called to marriage'. Applying all that I have argued I would say that it's a catchall rule that misses the human element. If I were writing a paragraph on the subject for the Sermon on the Mount, it might go like this. 'You have heard it said of old time 'Abstinence is right for those not called to marriage', but I say unto you whoever fails to show love and respect in relationship has committed fornication'? In other words, the moral essence of the teaching is that quality of relationship is even more important than restrictions of relationship such as no sex before marriage or no gay sex.

If I were to go round the Junior Common Rooms of Oxford sticking up notices that said, 'Abstinence is right for those not called to marriage', they'd be ridiculed and defaced. But if, on the other hand, I were to put up notices saying something like 'Relationship = Love and Respect', which I think is an even more deeply Christian ethical insight, I am confident that the defacement level would fall, and that a lot of students would inwardly nod and take note.

Other faiths

We have already discussed this when considering whether Christianity is inclusive or exclusive. Since 11 September 2001 the question has been more focused.
Many would wish to interpret the events of that day and all that they imply as a
war between Islam and the West, and since America is a largely Christian country, that tension could equally be described as a war between Islam and Christianity. Should Christians seek to convert people of other faiths to their point
of view, as some would argue, for the sake of their immortal souls? Or should
Christians make a point of learning about other faiths in order to understand
their spiritual gifts? The way of reconciliation certainly suggests the latter and
that would be the liberal approach. The aim would be to honour one another
within a framework of mutual respect.

For the liberal Christian mind it is not a priority to convert others to one's
point of view. If people are drawn to Christian faith by what they see and hear,
so much the better, but godliness does not have to conform to any particular
formula.

Having said that, I remember how when I was first a vicar my bishop said
that his aim was to 'convert the whole of North London'. I really admired him
for that and his exuberant exaggeration. To have proposed anything less would
have been half-hearted and weedy, but I knew that he didn't mean that I was to
set about trying to convert the large number of Jews living in my parish. This
grandiose ambition was an affirmation of confidence in the good news of the
gospel that was entrusted to both of us.

Women

In the Anglican Communion this is primarily an issue for the Church of England, most of the other provinces including America and Australia having accepted the priestly and episcopal ministry of women some time ago. Of course,
for the Roman Church it remains an unresolved matter. It just seems logical
that any Church that ordains women to the priesthood should also ordain
women as bishops. I only wish that some of the women priests who argue for it
were not so strident or so self-evidently ambitious for power.

Biblical literalism

I have become tedious on this question, I know, but it is in my view the issue that most divides the Christian Church. You could say that the Church is not so much divided into denominations as into those who take the Bible literally and those who don't. Blood could still be spilled over this one, but in all these areas Christians need to live and let live in order to free the Church to attend to society's hot potatoes: the ethics of war and bombing, the environment, the rich poor divide, violence, education, medical ethics and health, provision for old people, genetic engineering, and scandals affecting the church such as paedophilia amongst priests.

12.

Perfect freedom

In the great Chapter Eight of his Letter to the Romans, St Paul claims that God has set him free from 'the law of sin and death' through Christ Jesus. Later he moves on from the personal to the universal by claiming that creation itself will be set free from its bondage to decay and obtain the glorious liberty of the children of God. This glorious liberty is the 'perfect freedom' of my title. It is much more than democratic freedom or individual liberty; it is a subtle freedom of the spirit, that isn't always pain free, but nevertheless leads to happiness and the deep-down contentment of Christianity.

To explore it further I want to start by asking what needs Christianity meets in us. My publisher asks me this question. He wants straight answers; he wants to get down to the nitty gritty; he wants to know, as he says, where the rubber hits the road. Putting aside the fact that I always seek to flatter him, it seems to me a very good question. I might express it another way; how does Christianity make us free?

A power-greater-than-ourselves

When I raised the issue – what needs does Christianity meet – as a discussion topic at my annual Parish Conference, one of the first responses was from a man who said that for him it satisfies a deep spiritual longing. This idea was quickly taken up by a woman who described how God upholds her life. These immediate replies matched what I had put at the top of my own list: the need for a power-greater-than-ourselves, which is satisfied by God.

Belief in God helps us see ourselves in perspective within the vast expanse of the universe. The universe is essentially a lonely place: astrophysicists say that there is as much matter in the universe as three grains of sand in an empty cathedral. That means that if all the stars in all the galaxies and solar systems were pressed together they would only add up to three grains in an empty cathedral. I find that a scary thought. If there is so little stuff in such a vast space, what is the likelihood of there being any meaning linking it together? And doesn't it make our life, which seems so important to us, almost totally insignificant in the grand scale of things? But belief in a personal God who is the transcendent source of all being meets that anxiety. God is like an infinitely elastic quality of relationship stretching beyond and around the limits of human experience and knowledge acting as a force of integration and unity, binding matter and meaning together.

That is my way of putting it. It is, I suppose, a version of what theology calls justification by grace through faith. John Barton, the Professor of Old Testament at Oxford, says that he understands justification by faith to 'have to do with one's sense of being grasped by God through an act which owes everything to God and nothing to one's own efforts'. This idea of being freely supported and sustained by God is immensely liberating.

Community

The second need identified at the parish conference, and the one that was mentioned more than any other, was community. People said how much they valued the support that they got from friendships and activities at church. Most churches have a communal and social side, ranging from mother and toddler groups to youth clubs and badminton clubs to discussion groups. It's easy to mock the social seductions of the parish hall but they provide the venue for many enjoyable and rewarding activities, some of which are a lifeline to people who would otherwise be quite isolated.

Community is also about worship, the central act of which is the Holy Communion where worshippers share bread and wine together in remembrance of Jesus' Last Supper with his disciples. It draws on that most fundamentally unifying social activity, eating together. So that at the heart of the Church is this constant reminder that Christianity is a communal religion based on friendship and relationship, not a private hobby.

That is terribly important because Christian community is not about being a private club, but about breaking down barriers and bringing people together.

One person said that he belonged to many different groups and networks, but what was special about the Christian community was that it built relationships across barriers of class, wealth, ability, and race.

The building blocks of community are our relationships. Some people are too shy and others too macho to admit their need for love, but we all crave it. If we have no love and no relationship there's a real danger of going mad, as anyone who has had to endure solitary confinement will tell you. Relationship is one of the principal sources of meaning in our lives and most of our problems arise from messing up in the relationship department, both at the personal and political levels. Good relationships bring freedom because they release us to be ourselves.

Christianity meets the need for relationship in two ways. First by showing us how to accept and cherish one another at the personal level – a skill that Jesus was particularly good at and that he taught through parables such as the Good Samaritan. This Christian art of love even has its own word, agape – a rather ugly word as it happens with the beautiful meaning of un-self-interested love. This is a love unencumbered by the passions of eroticism, which can be so self-indulgent on the part of the lover who desires to possess and 'have' the beloved. Agape by contrast pays concentrated attention to the beloved, seeing them with a care and vision unobscured by the ego. George Herbert attributed this virtue to Christ in a poem about the soul entering the heavenly banquet, in which he described Christ as 'quick-ey'd love'. The soul enters the room and feels, as anyone might, shy and uncomfortable, but Christ immediately sees the problem and 'sweetly questioning' asks 'if I lacked anything'. This love is attentive, instinctively understanding, and self-giving.

The second way Christianity meets the need for relationship is by assuring us that we are loved by God at the universal level. The Psalms express this big-time love of God with great confidence. Psalm 46 speaks of God as 'our refuge and strength, a very present help in trouble', and Psalm 23 refers to the fact that in the 'valley of the shadow of death' God's presence means I need 'fear no evil'.

It's a bold claim that needs a word of caution to avoid sentimentality. When I was a very young curate I preached a sermon called, 'Man's loneliness and God's answer'. A member of the congregation who had been a widow for 20 years told me it was romantic to suggest that God could solve the problem of loneliness – an invisible God could never be a substitute for the physical warmth and companionship of another person. I never forgot that advice, but it doesn't disprove the existence of universal love. To be loved by God is to have an indelible place in the grand scheme whether you live or die. To be loved by God is to matter, to have meaning, to exist. As Jesus says, 'Are not five sparrows sold for two pennies? Yet not one of them is forgotten in God's sight. Do not be afraid; you are of more value than many sparrows.'

Purpose

The third need to be identified, after God and community, was purpose. It was summed up by the person who said that she looked to Christianity for guidance and a path through life. Someone else said that it provides a framework for living and goals and standards to aspire to. But the comment I liked best, referring to the Church, was simply, 'This is where I go to make sense of the world'

This clearly has a lot in common with the need for God, and particularly the moral framework that God gives to life. God helps people shape their priorities and answer the teasing questions about what ultimately matters and what is worth living for? Christianity satisfies this need by providing a moral base and advice on what leads to fulfilment, such as putting others first and not worrying about material possessions.

One of my parishioners argued that 'people functioning at a high level are totally lost ethically'. This discussion took place at the time of the Enron and Worldcom scandal in America, when it was discovered that billions of dollars profit had been falsely claimed by fraudulent accounting. He was generalising from the particular and while it would be absurd to say that all people functioning at a high level are ethically lost, there is undoubtedly a feeling that something is rotten at the heart of capitalism, which we need liberating from. Modern capitalism developed in the Christian cultures of Europe and America, and yet Mammon seems to have got the better of God despite the professed Christian faith of many of the national leaders.

The discussion on purpose concluded with the claim that the Bible is an important foundation on which to build a liberated life. I think it's fair to say that everyone present would read the Bible as literature and not interpret the text literally or invest it with divine authority. Revealing of God's purposes? Yes. Directly given by God? No. Yet it was clearly seen to have pivotal importance. The key claim was that the Bible is a source of narratives that reflect our lives. What does that mean? It means that we are able to recognise in the stories of the Bible our own spiritual and moral quest. The experience of Jacob, Job, Simon Peter or the fictional anti-hero of the 'Prodigal Son' is also our experience. We are therefore able to measure ourselves against these stories as if we were taking two pictures, one of ourselves and one from the Bible, and super-imposing them on one another to see how they match. But more than that, the best of the Bible stories encourage spiritual development by entering a sort of dialogue with the reader. You don't simply read about the sacrifice of Isaac, or the crucifixion of Christ, or the Good Samaritan and take it or leave it. The story becomes part of your mental furniture, part of the mental environment you inhabit. You are forced to think, to reconsider your position, to enter into dialogue with the text. These are stories that can change your life. The only problem is that these days not many people read the Bible and the stories that were once familiar to the population at large are now widely unknown. That's why one of our group said that we need the confidence to tell Christianity as a story.

The truth will set you free

But what would that story be? The heart of it, obviously, must be the story of Jesus. In this book I have based my argument primarily on impressions of his life because to me that life is both the essential Christianity and also the story of freedom. It communicates and oozes a sense of freedom, but never defines what it is – because stories don't define. His *bon mot* to the Pharisees, after being accused of breaking the Sabbath, is the nearest we get to definition, 'The Sabbath was made for man, not man for the Sabbath'. Yet Jesus was not anti-law, or anti-society; he was a bit of a maverick who said provocative things to wind people up theologically so that they were able to be more creative in their spiritual response. Provocation is a necessary part of the gospel. Why do so many sermons send us to sleep? Usually because they are totally uncontroversial, bland and unexceptionable. People want to go away from a sermon inspired to think, and for that to happen the preacher has got to be prepared to take risks, but most preachers are afraid to do so lest they be accused of rocking the boat or blaspheming the 'truth'. Jesus was often accused of blasphemy and if he hadn't been, probably not many people would have taken any notice of him.

There's a story of a churchwarden from a very conservative church who attended a meeting addressed by a radical theologian. The theologian questioned the conventional Christian approach to the Bible and theology. At the end of the talk the churchwarden put up his hand and said to the speaker, 'I just want to thank you for putting so clearly the things that I have secretly believed for a long time, but daren't tell my vicar for fear of offending him'. Unbeknown to the churchwarden, the vicar had slipped in late at the back and he stood up and said, 'That's funny, John, because I have never said these things for fear of offending you'.

Jesus' freedom, as we have noted repeatedly, is not restricted to what he says, but is evident in his actions: he abandoned his family to lead a peripatetic life, mixing with social outcasts, with women and children, and performing signs that break the social mould: healing lepers and madmen, and taking the ultimate risk of returning to the political/religious cauldron of Jerusalem to face the wrath of his opponents – the very ones who accused him of blasphemy.

That life has had its impact on history. At several points we have seen how Christianity addresses the need for freedom: actual physical freedom for captives and the politically oppressed, freedom from the destructive consequences of sin, freedom to pursue intellectual and theological questioning, wherever it may lead. Jesus said that to follow his words would help a person to 'know the truth, and the truth will make you free.'

Despite many blots on the landscape of its history – the aforementioned Crusades and the Spanish Inquisition – Christianity is a religion of liberation and liberty. Christians campaigned for the abolition of slavery, for civil rights in America, for the end of apartheid in South Africa, against the communist repression in Russia and Czechoslovakia, for education and welfare for the poor in 19th-century Britain.

'Liberal' and 'Christianity' are therefore words that belong together because God wants humanity to be free: he allows free will, forgives sins, and is open-handed in the generosity of creation.

Perhaps, therefore, the question, 'What needs does Christianity meet?' can be answered with one word, the need for freedom. The answers given in my parish discussion could all come under this head: the need for God, for community, for purpose, for love. In addition we identified one more fundamental liberty that Christianity provides – the freedom from the burden of sin. We didn't express it quite so theologically. It was said that Christianity can set you free from the weight of those earthly things that pull you back, such as guilt, love of wealth, injustice, and the anxieties of modern living.

Freedom from guilt

In modern British society guilt is not a word you hear very often. Indeed, it might seem an old-fashioned concept. We live in an impenitent age of individualism and breakdown of communal responsibility, where the consensus is that a person should be free to do their own thing and not be too bothered about how it affects others. This is the 'anything goes' morality of secular liberalism, which is not the kind of freedom I advocate or see as a part of Christian Liberalism. Christian freedom carries duties – namely, to love God and your neighbour as yourself – and freedom grows out of that discipline of Christian love.

The prayers of confession in the liturgies of the past 30 years are broadly apologetic in tone, speaking rather blandly of sinning 'in thought, word and deed', whereas in those of the older Book of Common Prayer the congregation says, 'we have offended against thy holy laws … and there is no health in us', and at Holy Communion, 'we acknowledge and bewail our manifold sins and wickedness'… the burden of which is 'intolerable'. When I was a theological student and the new prayers were first coming in, it was thought that the confessions of the Book of Common Prayer represented an unhealthy grovelling before God of a kind that might induce a psychologically damaging sense of guilt. This was the age of Freud not Henry VIII. So confession was watered down. It might have fitted with the spirit of the age, but it fails to do justice to the theological need for penitence. I suspect that modern society might be impenitent but it is not guilt free. People might not think twice about the damage they do to the environment when they buy flown-in-from-Africa vegetables from a supermarket, but the guilt of hurting a lover or failing your child can still cut deep. Underneath the surface of the go-for-it, live-for-the-moment, culture conscience can still prick and unresolved guilt has a debilitating effect.

As we saw in the Chapters on Prayer and Salvation, God offers a new start to anyone who genuinely seeks forgiveness. The great strength of this forgiveness is of course that it depends on God rather than human impulse, and that coming from God it has a force and authority that can effectively wipe the slate clean. In the universal scale of God's love, sin can be absorbed in a way that allows for renewal.

Putting money in perspective

A few years ago I decided to make an investment in property development. It was a risk that my friends advised against, but I was fed up with letting my house to students who repeatedly lost the keys to their rooms and smashed in the doors and ran up heavy telephone bills on sex calls. I wanted an easier way of building up security for my retirement. So I put my trust in an investment company whose chairman I had got to know. The plan was simple: we would borrow money, buy a building in Glasgow, turn it into luxury flats and sell them on for a profit. All seemed to be going well until one day he phoned to ask me to meet him in the Randolph Hotel in Oxford where he told me that he was bankrupt and the company was about to be placed in the hands of the receiver. He assured me that I would be all right and, although I felt sick in the pit of my stomach, the priest in me came to the fore and I tried to offer him some sort of comfort. Three weeks later he was dead, owing many millions of pounds.

The effect on me was deeply shocking: I couldn't sleep, was constantly on edge and thought I would have a breakdown. The only good outcome seemed to be that my congregation found my sermons more engaging than usual. In grappling with my own problems I had inadvertently begun to grapple with theirs. Not that they all had financial problems, but my personal crisis made me think more deeply and more carefully about spiritual priorities, in which I kept coming back to my favourite of Jesus' sayings, that where your treasure is, there will your heart be also. My treasure was literally at a very vulnerable place and therefore my heart was much more sympathetic than usual with human vulnerability. I remember that my first sermon after that meeting in the Randolph coincided with a massive economic crisis in Russia and we had seen heart-rending news pictures of Russians queuing outside banks in the hope of rescuing their savings. In the same news bulletins we had seen pictures of young men and women in the Sudan who had had limbs blown off by landmines, hopping around on crutches. Reflecting on all this I said that day, 'suddenly it comes home to you how fragile life is, how vulnerable people are, what a bloody business life is for so many people, and how love, hospitality, compassion, fidelity, refusing to love money, contentment, and sharing are essential aspects not only of the Christian life but also of survival.'

I found genuine liberation in the realisation that the values that ultimately matter are relational and spiritual rather than material. For example, you can have a fine house and smart cars and a large bank balance, but if you've no one to share it with you will still be unhappy. In the scale of wealth, happiness increases with bigger income only at the bottom end of the scale – the sector between abject poverty and sufficient food, housing and clothing. Above that point material add-ons increase happiness less and less: two cars do not make you twice as happy as one and greater wealth can sometimes have a negative effect on happiness because of the increased worry it brings.

It is obvious in our society that wealth creates social divisions and birds of a feather tend to flock together, whether it's in poor housing estates or luxury developments, private or state schools, 'economy' or first class travel, VIP lounges or hostels for the homeless. In the Christian community these barriers can and ought to be broken down, importantly by Christians working for social justice, but even more importantly by Christian people simply living together in communal relationship where these very superficial divisions are not allowed to matter. I have seen this levelling effect in practice in our ecumenical drop-in centre for the homeless, where friendships and relationships of trust build up between people struggling with street poverty and addiction and volunteers from 'well-to-do' North Oxford homes. That is an example from a conjunction of extreme social situations, but it is indicative of what is possible. I have been impressed by the open handed, unaffected ability of so many people to see others as persons and children of God rather than successes or failures on the slippery ladder of materialism.

So Christianity meets the need for freedom by helping us to get the issue of wealth in perspective. Both Jesus and my wife had the same advice to give me after my flirtation with big business – Don't worry! As Jesus put it, 'do not worry about your life, what you will eat or what you will drink, or about your body, what you will wear. Is not life more than food, and the body more than clothing?'

Injustice

Christianity at its best reminds us of the pressing need for social justice. Jesus himself stands in the prophetic tradition of Isaiah and Amos, who condemned those who exploited the poor and needy to build their fine houses. Jesus says in his manifesto in Luke 4, that God had 'anointed him to bring good news to the poor and liberty to the captive'. This was a theme that Luke had already introduced in the first chapter of his gospel where, as we noted in chapter 4, the Virgin Mary says that God 'has put down the mighty from their seat and exalted the humble and meek' and that he has filled the hungry with good things and sent the rich away empty. This is the so-called 'bias to the poor' of the gospel message.

In response, Christians have worked against injustice by establishing aid agencies such as 'Christian Aid', and organisations to help children, prisoners, the homeless, the elderly, the sick and oppressed. They have campaigned for peace, against nuclear weapons, for women's rights, for gay rights, for the cancellation of Third World debt, for asylum seekers, and prisoners of conscience. Christianity doesn't remove the problem of injustice – that would be a romantic dream – but it does provide a theology for liberation: namely, that the other person always matters! Human beings are made in the image of God and are therefore not only made equal, but equally to be honoured; friend and enemy, rich and poor, male and female, black and white, young and old.

The effect of 'globalisation' and instant news has made us more aware of injustice, yet, ironically, more indifferent or insensitive to it, as TV images flick from horror to scandal, to sport and back again. Three things stand out in my mind in the global culture: the degree of inequality between rich and poor nations, the tribal feuds between peoples, and the level of cruelty perpetrated by human beings on each other. There is always horror somewhere in the world: one only has to mention Rwanda, Bosnia, Kosovo, Afghanistan, Iraq, or Northern Ireland to have a clue about what is going on. The cruelty is unspeakable, or I should say often unspoken about, in the sense that much of it goes unreported and is only obliquely referred to in news bulletins, whether it is a sectarian attack in Belfast or a young man beaten with base ball bats before being nailed to a fence, the cutting up of babies with machetes in the ethnic cleansing of the Tutsis by the Hutu in Rwanda, or the castration and other sexual mutilations of prisoners in Afghanistan. The Christian discourse on justice usually takes place in a more genteel vocabulary and with more anodyne illustrations. But if provocation is a necessary part of the gospel, it is certainly a necessary part of the protest against global injustice because the further we distance ourselves from the specifics of cruelty and violence, the more tolerable it becomes. The prophetic voice of liberation must speak provocatively against the root causes of violence and cruelty, which are very often related to the exploitation of the weak by the strong.

So, how does Christianity play its part in political liberation? First by example, particularly in the lives of saints and martyrs. Secondly by its prophetic persistence in defending the poor and marginalized, and questioning the morality of oppression, including war. Thirdly by thinking about the nature of liberty. For example, by the strict application of the insight that all people matter; people need to be liberated not only from having violence done to them, but from having to do violence. The sinner as well as the sinned against matter to God and the Christian gospel seeks to set at liberty both the exploiter and exploited. The Campaign for Fair Trade is a model for this (although in my context the example might seem as weak as the tea it sometimes produces!). Third World farmers who are exploited by the economic muscle of the First World deserve a fair price for their crop; fair trading can benefit both producer and consumer. One is liberated economically, the other is liberated morally. Freedom is revolutionary and a settled church tied down by convention needs to remember this.

The peace of God

One of the last responses to my question was from a woman who said that she comes to church because it's a chance to stop in a busy world. She wanted to find release from the stress and pressure of modern life. Well, I'm not one to go in for spiritual quackery, but I do think that Christianity offers inner calm even if it doesn't iron out all the stress wrinkles. In his farewell to the disciples in John's Gospel, Jesus said, 'my peace I give you; not as the world gives give I to you'. Quite what this peace is is always hard to define and Paul famously commented that the peace of God 'passeth all understanding'. In fact I think it is to do with contentment, acceptance of how things are, gratitude for gifts received, a sense of proportion, and the ability not to worry about material things.

This is the paradox of world and spirit all over again. The peace of God passes all understanding not because it's a riddle wrapped up in an enigma, but because it is found where you least expect it – in Jesus' upside down values of the last being first and losing your life to save it.

I recently heard a radio programme in which disabled people were discussing, from a Christian point of view, how faith helped them to cope with disability. Their principal argument was that God has given us the gift of life and each of us has different physical and intellectual attributes; the important thing is gratefully to accept who you are and to build on the gifts you've been given. It is no good always wishing that circumstances were different, that you were able to do this or that, because that is the path to resentment and misery. You have to concentrate on what you can do, can enjoy, can contribute to society. That struck me as an approach to life that all of us would benefit from adopting. It reminded me of the much-quoted bit of etymology that the verb to heal is from the same root as whole – to heal is to make whole – and that in the gospels, when Jesus heals the blind, the deaf, and the lame, he is not just concerned with the physical condition of his patients, but with their spiritual condition, because to be fulfilled, to be whole, is more about attitude of mind than the body beautiful.

As St Paul said in the Letter to the Galatians, those who live according to the flesh set their minds on the things of the flesh, but those who live according to the Spirit set their minds on the things of the Spirit. That spiritual attention is what brings inner calm and to have peace of mind makes you free.

Whose service is perfect freedom?

The first task of any priest is to mediate the wonder and transcendence of God. It sounds a tall order. Who is capable of making such revelation? Let me put it another way. The first task of any priest is to make people aware of their need of God, because, as Pascal implied when he wrote, 'you would not be looking for Me if you did not already possess Me', to seek God is also to find him.

What I have been trying to argue in this book about liberal Christianity is summed up by that line; freedom is to know one's need of God and to respond to it. I realise this is not a unique 'liberal' insight; why should it be? God, Christ, and Human Response are part of the Christian equation whichever way you come at it, but there are different methods of making the calculation: conservative, liberal, evangelical, catholic, orthodox, devout sceptic. I call my method liberal.

The bottom line is, I think, that we can never be entirely happy by our selves. We are dependent creatures who need human community, but in addition we actually need to relate to a power greater than ourselves, and to acknowledge that power, to be comfortable and happy in our relationships and with everything else. Without that greater power to draw on (and in religious language to 'worship and adore') we're always subject to our own desires, which can obscure our vision, distort our judgement, and dispossess us of our freedom.

A priest who tries to mediate the wonder and transcendence of God often turns to poetry. Early on I referred to religion as 'this wonderful mythic, symbolic, poetic system that's about deep truth', but I have tried to put things first hand in my own words rather than using other people's. However, my final point is made by the Welsh priest and poet R S Thomas in a poem entitled, 'The Kingdom'. He is referring to what Jesus calls the kingdom of God, which is not a place but more an attitude of mind. He says,

> 'It's a long way off but inside it
> There are quite different things going on:
> … mirrors in which the blind look
> At themselves and love looks at them
> Back; and industry is for mending
> The bent bones and the minds fractured
> By life …
> … admission
> Is free, if you will purge yourself
> Of desire, and present yourself with
> Your need only and the simple offering
> Of your faith, green as a leaf.